SOCIAL INFRASTRUCTURE AND VULNERABILITY IN THE SUBURBS

Lucia Lo, Valerie Preston, Paul Anisef, Ranu Basu, and Shuguang Wang

Social Infrastructure and Vulnerability in the Suburbs examines how the historically low-density, car-centric geography of outer suburbs and the entrenchment of neoliberal governance in the past several decades have affected disadvantaged populations in North American metropolitan areas. Taking the prime example of York Region, a large outer suburb north of Toronto, the authors analyse patterns of demographic change and vulnerability in the suburbs.

The volume looks at use of and access to support services by vulnerable groups who are not traditionally associated with the suburbs: recent immigrants, seniors, and low-income families. Providing empirical evidence on four types of public infrastructure – education, employment, housing, and settlement services – this book also presents a range of policy recommendations on how to address the social inequalities that characterize these rapidly growing suburban areas.

LUCIA LO is a professor in the Department of Geography at York University.

VALERIE PRESTON is a professor in the Department of Geography at York University.

PAUL ANISEF is a professor emeritus in the Department of Sociology at York UNIVERSITY.

RANU BASU is an associate professor in the Department of Geography at York University.

SHUGUANG WANG is a professor in the Department of Geography at Ryerson University.

Social Infrastructure and Vulnerability in the Suburbs

Lucia Lo, Valerie Preston, Paul Anisef, Ranu Basu, and Shuguang Wang

UNIVERSITY OF TORONTO PRESS
Toronto Buffalo London

© University of Toronto Press 2015
Toronto Buffalo London
www.utppublishing.com
Printed in the U.S.A.

ISBN 978-1-4426-5024-4 (cloth)
ISBN 978-1-4426-2832-8 (paper)

Printed on acid-free, 100% post-consumer recycled paper with vegetable-based inks.

Library and Archives Canada Cataloguing in Publication

Lo, Pui-Chun Lucia, 1948–, author
Social infrastructure and vulnerability in the suburbs/Lucia Lo, Valerie Preston,
Paul Anisef, Ranu Basu, and Shuguang Wang.

Includes bibliographical references and index.
ISBN 978-1-4426-5024-4 (bound). – ISBN 978-1-4426-2832-8 (pbk.)

1. Infrastructure (Economics) – Ontario – Toronto Suburban Area.   2. Neoliberalism –
Economic aspects – Ontario – Toronto Suburban Area.   3. Neoliberalism – Social
aspects – Ontario – Toronto Suburban Area.   4. Human geography – Ontario – Toronto
Suburban Area.   5. Toronto Suburban Area (Ont.) – Economic policy.   6. Toronto
Suburban Area (Ont.) – Social policy.   I. Preston, Valerie A., author   II. Anisef, Paul,
1942–, author   III. Basu, Ranu, 1964–, author   IV. Wang, Shuguang, 1956–, author
V. Title.

HC118.T6L64 2015   338.9713'547   C2014-907613-4

This book has been published with the help of a grant from the Federation for the
Humanities and Social Sciences, through the Awards to Scholarly Publications Program,
using funds provided by the Social Sciences and Humanities Research Council of Canada.

University of Toronto Press acknowledges the financial assistance to its publishing
program of the Canada Council for the Arts and the Ontario Arts Council, an agency of
the Government of Ontario.

   Canada Council   Conseil des Arts   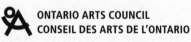   ONTARIO ARTS COUNCIL
for the Arts   du Canada   CONSEIL DES ARTS DE L'ONTARIO

University of Toronto Press acknowledges the financial support of the Government of
Canada through the Canada Book Fund for its publishing activities.

Contents

Tables

Figures

Acknowledgments

The research reported in this book was funded by a research grant from Infrastructure Canada and the Social Sciences and Humanities Research Council of Canada and by a financial contribution from Citizenship and Immigration Canada, Ontario Region. Also crucial to the completion of this project was support from York University's Office of the Vice-President, Research and Innovation; the former Faculty of Arts; and the current Faculty of Liberal Arts and Professional Studies. The views expressed herein are the views of the authors and do not represent the views of the Government of Canada or York University.

In conducting this research project, we partnered with the Human Services Planning Coalition of York Region, a network of governmental and non-governmental organizations, and benefited tremendously from the participation of its member organizations in our consultative workshops and their commitment to addressing the needs of York Region's vulnerable populations.

The Institute of Social Research at York University helped to administer the survey. We are grateful for the very capable assistance provided by its associate director, David Northrup, and his staff. A number of community organizations in York Region helped to recruit participants for the survey in its second phase. They included, but were not limited to, COSTI, Human Endeavour, Welcome Centre Immigrant Services, Sanatan Mandir Cultural Centre, Jewish Immigrant Aid Services, Community and Home Assistance to Seniors, Catholic Community Services of York Region, Social Enterprise, Unity Club, Formosa Evergreen Senior Citizens Centre, Vishnu Temple, and Friuli Terrace.

Our project manager, Etta Anisef, and our financial manager, Joan Broussard, provided exceptional organizational expertise. Silvia

D'Addario, James McLean, Ann Marie Murnaghan, and Yinhuan Yuan, former graduate students in the Department of Geography at York University, offered capable research assistance at different stages of the project. We are particularly grateful to Ann Marie who, years after she had left York University, graciously agreed to reproduce all the maps accompanying this volume; her assistance went well above and beyond.

We thank Douglas Hildebrand of the University of Toronto Press for believing in the value of the book; the three anonymous readers for their thoughtful comments and suggestions, which helped us to strengthen the manuscript; and Philippa Campsie for her editorial assistance in the first draft of this book. Lucia Lo and Valerie Preston want to acknowledge the encouragement and support from their spouses, Cedric Ng and Joe Cox, respectively, who got them through the home stretch as the manuscript came to fruition.

The completion of the manuscript coincided with the birth of Cameron Han-Chi Taylor and gives Lucia more time to attend to and enjoy precious moments with her grandson. Lucia dedicates this book to the future of little Cameron and his generation. In a similar manner Paul dedicates this book to his granddaughter, Sabine Scout Anisef, born when our last task – reading and correcting the proofs – was due. Ranu, Shuguang, and Valerie dedicate the book to their children, Rohan, Vivek, Jai, Simon, and Elizabeth, with the hope that they will live in a just society.

SOCIAL INFRASTRUCTURE AND VULNERABILITY IN THE SUBURBS

1 Vulnerability and Neoliberalism in the Suburbs

In contemporary societies, where individuals are increasingly responsible for their own well-being, equitable access to public infrastructure plays a crucial role in ensuring that all citizens can participate fully in society (Beck 1993; Graham and Marvin 2001; McFarlane and Rutherford 2008). All types of public infrastructure – physical infrastructure such as transportation systems, water, sewer, and other utilities; health infrastructure; amenities such as parks and recreational services; knowledge-based infrastructure such as education facilities and libraries; and social services such as settlement services, affordable housing, and employment services – influence the inclusion of urban residents. This is particularly true for vulnerable groups such as the elderly who have limited mobility, the poor who lack financial resources, and newly arrived immigrants who need specialized information and support services (Cutter 2003). The needs of these populations are sometimes difficult to meet in new suburban areas where rapid population growth outstrips the capacity of the existing infrastructure (Collin and Poitras 2002; Wolch, Pastor, and Dreier 2004). Unmet needs in the rapidly urbanizing outer suburbs heighten social exclusion as income gaps grow and civic engagement falls to historical lows (Brodie 2007; Graham and Marvin 2001; Millington 2011, 2012).

Three trends heighten the imbalance between the supply of infrastructure and the need for infrastructure in many contemporary outer suburbs. First, with a short history of development, outer suburban areas have been particularly vulnerable to the full impact of fiscal constraint at all levels of government in the past two decades. As neoliberalism has taken root, governments have reduced spending on all forms of infrastructure, physical and social, by restricting their investments in new services and in the operation of existing services (England and Ward 2007; Peck 2010). Without the historical legacy of investment found in the older parts of metropolitan areas, new suburbs have suffered a large shortfall in infrastructure relative to other locations (Bunting, Walks, and Filion 2004; Clutterbuck and Howarth 2002; Keil and Young 2009; Suttor 2007).

Second, infrastructure demands are increasing rapidly in suburban areas where vulnerable populations are growing in number and as a proportion of the total population. Residents are aging in place; economic restructuring is leaving behind many suburban residents and swelling the numbers of low-income households in the suburbs; and growing numbers of new immigrants are settling directly in the suburbs, outside the traditional reception areas at the centre of metropolitan areas (Alba, Logan, Stults, Marza, and Zhang 1999; Boudreau, Keil, and Young 2009; Lo and Wang 1997; Marcelli 2004; Murdie and Teixeira 2003).

Third, automobile-oriented, low-density, and highly segregated land-use patterns in the suburbs exacerbate public infrastructure needs. Residents must often travel long distances, using slow and infrequent public transportation (Graham 2000; Keil and Young 2008; McLafferty and Preston 1999) or driving through increasingly congested streets where travel speeds have recently declined (IBI Group 2009). To comply with zoning that separates residential land uses from all other types of land use, service providers often locate adjacent to industrial uses where land costs are low, thereby increasing travel distances.

In these contexts, this book examines in detail the availability of public infrastructure for vulnerable populations residing in a typical outer suburb and focuses on social infrastructure, that is, those services and programs that support a safe and healthy community and maintain and promote its quality of life. The key questions revolve around the geographies of social infrastructure and vulnerable populations. Primarily, how equitably is social infrastructure distributed in the outer suburbs? Is there an unmet need for social services among vulnerable populations? What can be done to minimize potential risks for these populations? The questions, asked and addressed in sequential order, are all related. They are intended to improve the understanding of and to help deal with the geographies of vulnerability in less-studied outer suburbs. The first question, focusing on the possibilities of physically accessing social infrastructure, is addressed by a comparison of the distribution of social infrastructure and the distribution of vulnerable populations, and the second question is approached by assessing the vulnerable groups' everyday awareness, use and satisfaction of services. The third, a policy-related question, aims to tackle some social exclusionary issues in suburbs.

The goal here is to contribute to recent debates about the changing nature and geographies of disadvantage in North American suburbs (Cisneros et al. 2009; Hanlon, Short, and Vicino 2009; Kneebone and Berube 2013; Young, Wood, and Keil 2011) by analysing a Canadian case. Canadian suburbs have emerged in distinct economic, social, and political contexts that have shaped their contemporary geographies (Harris 2004; Young, Wood, and Keil 2011). Recent commentators have emphasized that the current understanding of suburban development often rests on unacknowledged and unexamined assumptions of suburban homogeneity (Harris and Larkham 1999; Phelps and Wu 2011). In addition to the assumption that they are similar to one another, suburbs are also thought to be homogeneous in terms of their social and built characteristics. Despite a growing historical literature about the racial and class diversity of suburban populations (Harris and Larkham 1999; Harris 2004; Jackson 1985; Muller 1981, 1997; Silverstone 1997; Nicolaides and Wiese 2006), little research has specifically investigated their contemporary heterogeneity. Moreover, when the diversity of the suburbs is acknowledged, attention is focused on spatial structure, built form, and economic function, particularly compared with the gentrifying neighbourhoods close to the city centre (for example, Duany, Plater-Zyberk, and Speck 2001; Katz and Lang 2003; Stanilov and Scheer 2004; Teaford 2008). Relatively few studies pay attention to the people living in the suburbs, particularly the vulnerable populations.

This chapter reviews the current understanding of vulnerability and the crucial role of all types of infrastructure in mitigating it. Particular attention is paid to the impact of neoliberalism on the provision of infrastructure, noting that recent efforts to promote economically self-sufficient citizens and to operate government as a business may heighten social exclusion (Peck 2010). It then turns to the availability of infrastructure in contemporary suburbs that have been greatly affected by neoliberal policies.

Vulnerability and Infrastructure

Two bodies of work consider the impacts of infrastructure: the literature on social vulnerability and the literature on social inclusion and exclusion. Originating in the concept of a risk society, which takes as its starting point the idea that risk is induced by modernization or industrialization (Beck 1993; Giddens 1990), the literature on social vulnerability focuses on inequalities in experiences with and impacts of physical hazards and social risks (Cutter 2003). Vulnerability refers to the inability of people, organizations, and societies to withstand the adverse impacts of risks to which they are exposed. Whereas different socio-economic groups of a society may be similarly exposed to a specific physical hazard or social risk, they likely implement different strategies or actions to deal with the exposure. The risk would, accordingly, have varying consequences for groups with diverging capacities and abilities to handle the impact (Blaikie et al. 2005). In this regard, the social context in general and the social processes and structures in particular are important. The most significant factors are perhaps the economic, demographic, and political processes that affect the allocation and distribution of resources among different groups of people. In "liberal" welfare states such as the United States and Canada, market forces play a decisive role in the allocation of resources, often exacerbating disadvantage and vulnerability (Esping-Andersen 1990).

Some social groups are more vulnerable than others in the sense that they are less capable of mitigating risks. Disadvantaged individuals, such as seniors, the poor, the disabled, and many visible minorities, are particularly vulnerable. Bearers of multiple vulnerabilities are not uncommon. In Canada many members of visible minorities are recent immigrants, who find it difficult to obtain recognition of the credentials and work experience gained in their country of origin, with the result that they earn much less than do either Canadian-born workers or established immigrants, and they experience higher unemployment and poverty rates (Alboim, Finnie, and Meng 2005; Frenette and Morissette 2003; Hiebert 1999; Hou and Picot 2003; Ley and Smith 2000; Ornstein 2006; Picot and Hou 2003; Preston, Lo, and Wang 2003). Similarly, many seniors, living alone on a fixed income, may suffer from disabilities (The National Seniors Council 2009; Human Resources and Skills Development Canada, 2011).

The vicious cycle of vulnerability is difficult to overcome. Vulnerability persists because of structural influences inherent in social interactions, political institutions, and cultural values. Government devolution, and the continual process of downloading financial and logistical responsibility for social services, has led to further limitations in access to these services (Basu 2004; Hackworth and Moriah 2006; Keil 2002). Accessible social service infrastructure is, thus, a crucial means for reducing social inequalities in the exposure to risk and its impacts (DeBresson and Barker 1998).

Relations of power and powerlessness arising from, and embedded in, economic globalization, technological change, population migration, public-service restructuring, and discrimination produce deprivation, disadvantage, and exclusion among certain groups in societies. In recent decades the discourse on social exclusion and social inclusion has influenced the way we understand or attempt to change our world. On the academic front, this discourse has inspired a vast research and publication output. On the policy side, governments have attempted to adopt social inclusion as a guidepost for state policy agendas. Originating in France as a response to the growing signs of socio-economic strains such as resurgent unemployment and deepening poverty in Europe in the 1970s and 1980s, research on social exclusion and inclusion focuses on the barriers or lack of access that people encounter in their attempts to gain a share of society's resources (for example, Blackman, Brodhurst, and Convery 2001; Lucas 2004; Richmond and Saloojee 2005; Weiss 2003).

Generally, exclusion is seen as the problem, and inclusion as the solution (Roeher Institute 2003). Social exclusion refers to the denial of the right, or to the inability, of individuals or communities to participate fully in society because of any socially determined disadvantage (Willett 2003). Multiple and changing factors result in people being excluded from the normal exchanges, practices, and rights of modern society (Percy-Smith 2000). Conversely, social inclusion requires that every member of society be able to access its central goods, satisfy basic needs, and enjoy a reasonable quality of life (Gray 2000; Lucas 2004). A social-inclusion framework advocates "a broad equality of opportunities and life chances for individuals" and "the achievement of a basic level of well-being for all citizens" (Sen 2001). Social inclusion recognizes that a variety of conditions (such as discrimination and vulnerability based on age, gender, place of birth, income, or disability) exist and interact to exclude people from certain sub-populations.

Social exclusion involves both process and outcome. The processes of economic globalization, technological change, population migration, public-service restructuring, and discrimination unfold across space, rendering social exclusion an inherently spatial phenomenon (Gough and Eisenschitz with McCulloch 2006; Rose et al. 2013). Although national, regional, and municipal policies concerning transportation, housing, and social infrastructure mediate the effects of residential location, where one lives matters, particularly for vulnerable populations. In a comparative study of European cities Murie and Musterd (2004) found that residential location did not have a direct influence on the probability of falling into poverty, but it affected significantly the chances of escaping poverty.

The outcomes of social exclusion are multidimensional. Linkages are typically drawn between poverty and such issues as housing, health, education, crime, neighbourhood space, and access to services. Research in Canada has documented the social and spatial patterns of inclusion and exclusion within and across urban areas (Anisef and Lanphier 2003; Hulchanski 2010; Kazemipur and Halli 2000; Lee 2000; Ley and Smith 2000; Li 2003; Omidvar and Richmond 2003; Ornstein 2006; Walks 2011). Recent comparative research (Murie and Musterd 2004) has confirmed that welfare policies and infrastructure promote social inclusion by facilitating the participation of all members of society, regardless of their income, social identity, and residential location.

To summarize, both the social vulnerability literature and the social inclusion literature focus on the experiences and impacts of exposure to social inequality. Population vulnerability can be mitigated not only through public policies affecting income redistribution but equally by the availability of infrastructure, all processes that help to close the "physical, social and economic distances separating people" (Omidvar and Richmond 2003, ix).

Infrastructure in a Neoliberal Era

Recent literature emphasizes the impact of neoliberalism on infrastructure provision (Graham and Marvin 2001; Torrance 2008). As Larner (2000) notes, neoliberalism denotes a new form of political and economic governance premised on the extension of market relationships. From a Keynesian welfare state, where the provision of goods and services worked towards equity and social inclusion, the movement towards a neoliberal minimalist state is currently understood and accepted as the norm. The success of this ideological discourse, particularly during the past decade, has been hard to combat owing to the message of efficiency, accountability, and equity of resources that it conveys to the general electorate (Basu 2004; Boudreau, Keil, and Young 2009; Peck 2010).

The neoliberal project is inherently spatial (Brenner and Theodore 2002); its manifestation in and impacts on cities are readily apparent (Boudreau et al. 2007; Boudreau, Keil, and Young 2009; Leitner, Peck, and Sheppard 2007). *Neoliberalism as an ideology* in which ideals of marketization, privatization, and competition prevail has had serious effects that are tied closely to the way the urban form has been envisaged and planned in suburbs across North America. The transportation grid, for instance, was originally built towards an individualistic and automobile-oriented economy, rather than a transit system for the general public. Similarly neoliberal-directed marketization of property alongside the retrenchment of the welfare state meant that the residential landscape supported private property "boomtowns" rather than rental, cooperative, or social housing (Hackworth and Moriah 2006; Hackworth 2008). *Neoliberalism as a practice* is similarly reflected in the policies that developed in which services for vulnerable groups were not deemed necessary, were cut back, or were provided at a minimum level (Cowen 2005). When residents and communities were goaded to be self-reliant and less dependent on the state, the collective faltered. This is evident in the education system, where cultures of accountability and audit enforce close monitoring of performance and where education services provided through private and semi-private organizations are replacing public education.

The process of neoliberalizing the suburbs, or "neoliberal suburbanism" (see Peck 2011), has worked in spatially specific ways. Even before the twentieth century, suburban development was characterized often by profit-seeking private subdivision builders or developers, with governments not only failing to regulate transit or housing but also maintaining cosy relationships with private developers (Hayden 2003).[1] However, in the Fordist period following the Second World War, infrastructure was publicly provided at approximately equal cost to all residents. The shift to a post-Fordist urban economy, in which highly skilled workers concentrate in gentrified central neighbourhoods and less skilled workers are propelled to cheaper locations far from the centre, is associated with the private-sector provision of infrastructure (Millington 2011, 2012; Klausen and Røe 2012). The introduction of

---

1 As Harris (2004) points out, the activities of developers sometimes occurred in parallel with the suburbanization of self-help housing built by working-class owners.

variable prices for consumers affects vulnerable populations more than it does the affluent, and heightens the uneven spatial provision of infrastructure within contemporary urban areas. Infrastructure is provided primarily where the population can afford to pay for it. An example is Highway 407, the only toll road in the Greater Toronto Area that links many of the outer suburbs ringing the amalgamated city of Toronto (Torrance 2008). Although initial construction was funded by the provincial government, the toll road was sold to private investors largely to fulfil ideological commitments to privatization. With its high tolls the highway only facilitates the travel of the affluent, and the requirement that it continuously expand as volumes increase perpetuates reliance on the automobile. It has also transformed commuting patterns and promoted employment growth in the outer suburbs. For the first time, more people commute east–west across Toronto than travel to work in the city centre (Torrance 2008). Highway 407 exemplifies the way that privatization contributes to the social fragmentation and geographical "splintering" of contemporary urban areas (Graham and Marvin 2001; Teaford 2011; Young, Wood, and Keil 2011).

To date, however, research has focused on the physical, usually networked, infrastructure, investigating the utilities and transportation systems that underpin urban areas (Graham and Marvin 2001; Keil and Young 2008; Torrance 2008; Young and Keil 2010). In this respect the literature in Canada is similar to that in Europe and elsewhere where there has been relatively little research regarding the provision of social services and their effects on social exclusion, particularly in the rapidly growing outer suburbs (Klausen and Røe 2012; Millington 2011). Several Canadian studies have investigated the implications of government cutbacks and the downloading of responsibilities to local municipalities (for example, Frisken 2007; Frisken and Wallace 2002). Except for Basu (2002), Denton and Spencer (2001), Cowen (2005), Hackworth and Moriah (2006), Hackworth (2008), Lo (2011), Lo et al. (2007), Smoyer-Tomic et al. (2004), Truelove (2000), and Wang and Truelove (2003), little recent research has evaluated the access to infrastructure for different vulnerable populations in the current neoliberal Canadian context.

Suburbanization and Infrastructure in Canada

Suburbanization has enveloped much of the contemporary landscape, transforming social, built, and physical environments. Compared to city centres, suburbs are diversifying and growing much faster (Kopun

2007; Kopun and Keung 2007; Lo et al. 2007; Statistics Canada 2007c, 2012a), leading to concerns about suburban nations that, according to Duany, Plater-Zyberk, and Speck (2001) and their followers, not only have destroyed the traditional concept of the neighbourhood but have eroded vital social values such as equality, citizenship, and personal safety. Between 2001 and 2006 the growth rate of the peripheral municipalities of Canada's thirty-three census metropolitan areas (CMAs) was double the national average (11.1 per cent versus 5.4 per cent), whereas the central municipalities of those CMAs grew more slowly (at a rate of 4.2 per cent) than did the Canadian population as a whole, and less than half as fast as the peripheral municipalities (Statistics Canada 2007c). The Toronto Region is a telling example. In the same period, while population in the City of Toronto grew by 0.9 per cent, the population in some of the surrounding suburban municipalities grew by more than 20 per cent (for example, 33 per cent in Brampton, 31 per cent in Vaughan, 27 per cent in Whitby, and 25 per cent in Markham). This pattern of development in cities is typical of urban spread, which presents many challenges for the provision of social services.

It is hard to define a suburb, now that cities have become like suburbs and suburbs have become like cities (Jackson 2006). But because suburbs, especially outer suburbs, have a shorter history of development, they have been particularly susceptible to the full impact of the fiscal constraint associated with neoliberal policies in the past two decades (Boudreau, Keil, and Young 2009; Fiedler and Addie 2008; Frisken 2007; Peck 2001). In Ontario, the Canadian province that pioneered neoliberal policies under the banner of "the Common Sense Revolution," some of these policies have been reversed since 2003; however, the fiscal restraint and the ideologies associated with it persist.[2] In this context, the outer suburbs have suffered a larger shortfall in infrastructure than have other locations (Bunting et al. 2004; Clutterbuck and Howarth 2002). Meanwhile, population growth, accompanied by increasing diversity and social polarization (Alba et al. 1999; Marcelli 2004; Murdie and Teixeira 2003), has generated demands for additional infrastructure. Funding shortfalls, often related to provincial government downloading, have contributed to growing gaps between supply and

---

2 Uploading includes annual reductions in municipal responsibility for the administrative costs of social assistance and social assistance payments. In 2008 the provincial government agreed to upload $1.5 billion in annual costs related to provincial social services, court security, and road and bridge maintenance by 2018.

demand (PricewaterhouseCoopers LLP 2006). In Ontario the Province devolved responsibility for some social services to municipalities without contributing additional provincial funding (Boudreau, Keil, and Young 2008; Frisken 2007; Hackworth 2008).

The automobile-oriented, low-density, and highly segregated land-use patterns in the outer suburbs exacerbate infrastructure needs. Residents often have to travel long distances, using slow and infrequent public transportation, to reach a limited number of services (Graham 2000; Keil and Young 2008; McLafferty 1982; McLafferty and Preston 1992). Vulnerable populations such as recent immigrants, seniors, and the poor have been especially hard hit because they often rely on public transit (Banister and Bowling 2004; Blumenberg 2008; Blumenberg and Evans 2007; Church, Frost, and Sullivan 2000; Heisz and Schellenberg 2004; Hine and Mitchell 2001; Lo, Shalaby, and Alshalafah 2012).

Our understanding of the impacts of downloading on suburbs is limited because recent research about infrastructure has largely involved analyses of central cities that ignore the outer suburbs growing around them, or examinations of entire city regions that fail to distinguish suburbs from city centres. For example, studies by Hulchanski (2010), United Way of Greater Toronto and the Canadian Council on Social Development (2004), and Walks (2011) identify growing poverty in the inner suburbs of the city of Toronto . Outer suburbs that are central to the social, economic, and political functions of city regions are ignored. Similarly, the American research that has taken the suburb as the entry point of analysis focuses on the declining inner suburbs that boomed in the post-war period (Hanlon, Short, and Vicino 2009; Kneebone and Berube 2013; Lucy and Phillips 2000).

It is crucial to explore the services provided for vulnerable groups in Canada's outer suburbs. Some time ago, Bourne (1996) noted that the cost of suburban development extends beyond the physical and into the social infrastructure because "the socially disadvantaged, low-income minorities and elderly, single parents and some married women with young children, find themselves geographically isolated from both jobs and services" (173). The specific needs of these vulnerable groups have rarely been addressed (Chiras and Wann 2003). Friedman (2002) argued that planning regulations must be flexible to accommodate shifting societal demands and changing demographics, including a decline in the average family size, an aging population, and shifting work conditions. His discussion of flexible forms of housing and neighbourhoods, however, did not extend into specific discussions of seniors, immigrants, or low-income earners or the provision of "soft" services, such as education, employment, and settlement services. Whitzman (2006) rightly noted, for example, that changing demographics in the suburbs continue to outpace government responses, leading to a mismatch between the locations of demand and the locations of supply of services (see also Bunting et al. 2004).

While population growth in the suburbs has been faster than in the central city, there is a widespread misconception among both residents and policymakers that the affluence of suburban regions means that homelessness and other social problems that exist in the city are not present there. This unexamined assumption was evident in the decision that required regional municipalities in the Toronto area to contribute to a regional fund for social services. Even though the per capita spending on social services was lower in each of the regional municipalities than in the City of Toronto, the regional fund was used for facilities and agencies that served vulnerable populations in the City of Toronto (Frisken 2007).

A Case Study

The literature about suburbs mostly focuses on their evolution, their relation to the central city, and their subsequent decline. Attention is often paid to the inner suburbs or the in-between cities rather than to the outer suburbs that have developed recently. In a similar manner, where infrastructure – the core of urban development and the indicators of quality of life – is the focus, it is the hard, physical infrastructure such as highways and public transit that captures the interest. Social infrastructure such as housing, education, employment, and settlement services is seldom studied. This study addresses both of these shortcomings by analysing, in detail, the access to, awareness of, use of, and satisfaction with housing, education, employment, and settlement services in the Regional Municipality of York, commonly known as York Region, an exemplary outer suburb of the Toronto metropolitan region. While the next chapter situates York Region in its metropolitan context, we explain our choice of the case study area here.

With over five million people, Toronto is the largest metropolitan area in Canada. In comparison to Montreal and Vancouver, the second- and third-largest metropolitan regions, Toronto has the largest immigrant population and the most ethnic and racial diversity. For example, of the 1,110,000 newcomers who arrived in Canada between 2001 and

2006, 40.4 per cent went to Toronto, while 14.9 per cent chose Montreal and 13.7 per cent settled in Vancouver (Chui, Tran, and Maheux 2007). As a result, immigrants made up 45.7 per cent of the total population in the Toronto census metropolitan area, as opposed to 39.6 per cent of the population in the Vancouver CMA and 20.6 per cent in the Montreal CMA (Statistics Canada 2007a). The large influx of immigrants to Toronto has created what Vertovec (2007) describes as a super-diverse city where immigrants concentrate in specific locations, but many different ethno-cultural groups inhabit the same spaces. Toronto is home to immigrants from over two hundred ethnic origins. The influx of immigrants, especially in the economic class, also means that Toronto's population is generally younger, with a median age in 2006 of 37.5 years, compared to 39.3 and 39.1 years in Montreal and Vancouver respectively. The Toronto population is also wealthier and less reliant on government transfers than is the population in Montreal and Vancouver. Only 18.4 per cent of Toronto residents are considered to have low income, compared with 21.1 per cent and 20.8 per cent in Montreal and Vancouver respectively, and 8.1 per cent receive government transfers as part of their income, a lower percentage than in either Montreal or Vancouver (Statistics Canada 2007a). The Toronto metropolitan area was also the epicentre of neoliberal experiments in Ontario in the 1990s (Peck 2001). In addition to amalgamating six municipalities into the current City of Toronto,[3] the provincial government downloaded responsibility for several social services as well as provincial roads and other infrastructure, privatized municipal activities such as water testing, and established pooling so that the outer suburbs contributed to the costs of social services in the amalgamated City of Toronto (Peck 2001; Boudreau, Keil, and Young 2009). With its large, rapidly growing, and diverse population and its experience with neoliberal policies, metropolitan Toronto is an ideal laboratory for investigating the changing geography of vulnerability and social infrastructure in the outer suburbs.

The Toronto metropolitan area, commonly known as the Greater Toronto Area, consists of the City of Toronto and four regional municipalities – Durham Region to the east, York Region to the north, and Peel and Halton Regions to the west – that constitute the metropolitan area's

3 The amalgamation took place in 1998, and the six municipalities were East York, Etobicoke, North York, Scarborough, Toronto, and York.

outer suburbs. Etobicoke, North York, and Scarborough – the three former cities and boroughs bordering the Toronto city core and now part of the City of Toronto – are considered to be the inner suburbs of the metropolitan region. York Region stands out as an exemplar of the outer suburbs where rapid and diverse population growth has collided with neoliberal urban policies concerning infrastructure. Table 1.1 compares selected population characteristics of Toronto's outer suburbs in 2006. Of the four outer suburban regions, Peel Region and York Region were the largest with the largest numbers of immigrants and seniors. York Region has grown faster than has Peel Region in the last two decades when neoliberal policies predominated. It also has the second-highest proportion of low-income individuals and hosts some of the wealthiest neighourhoods in the metropolitan area (Cain 2013). In addition to these demographic characteristics, the timing and nature of development in York Region also render it particularly suitable for our investigation of infrastructure issues facing vulnerable populations in the outer suburbs. Development in York Region that emphasized the strict separation of residential and other land uses and the construction of expensive single-family housing units continued throughout the 1990s and early 2000s, as neoliberal policies took effect.

To understand the changing nature and roles of outer suburban areas in metropolitan regions, and to avoid repetition in the increasingly diverse outer suburbs of the decline that is happening to contemporary inner suburbs such as those in Toronto (Hulchanski 2010; Walks 2011), this study is a response to the recent call by Klausen and Røe (2012) for in-depth case studies. The age of neoliberalization has led to substantial disinvestment in urban social infrastructure, with the potential for negative impacts on the social foundations of our metropolitan regions. This case study argues that the unique suburban form of York Region – evident in population dispersal, the northern and southern density divide, the governance of urban-suburban-rural entities, the growth of tertiary-oriented economic activities, and increasing social polarization – has led to complex geographies of vulnerability in the neoliberal era. As Peck and Tickell (2002) note, the destructive "roll-back" and the creative moments of "roll-out" neoliberalism become evident in local neoliberalisms. In York Region, on the one hand, the roll-back of services has likely led to spatial mismatch in infrastructure provision. On the other hand, the roll-out of services is narrowly configured through ad hoc and patchwork programs that are unlikely to meet the needs of vulnerable populations in all parts of the region.

Table 1.1   Selected demographic characteristics of Toronto's suburban municipalities

	Durham	Halton	Peel	York
Total population, 2006	561,258	439,256	1,159,405	892,712
Population change, 1991–2006	37.0%	40.3%	58.2%	76.8%
Total immigrants, 2006	113,390	107,915	561,240	380,530
Immigrant growth, 1996–2006	32.2%	41.4%	65.4%	80.1%
Population 65+, 2006	60,155	54,840	104,525	91,920
Change in population 65+, 1996–2006	45.3%	46.5%	70.0%	88.6%
Population in low-income households, 2006	9.4%	8.4%	14.5%	12.7%

Source: Statistics Canada 2005b, 2007a

Although we do not adopt a governmentality approach to neoliberalism (Burchell, Gordon, and Miller 1991), the thrust of this study lies in unravelling the ways in which social inclusion, social exclusion, and vulnerability (and hence power and powerlessness) are produced and reproduced through the provision of infrastructure, which is defined and understood in non-traditional and multiple ways. Further, it attempts to dismantle the false illusion of York Region as solely an exurban suburb at the periphery of the Toronto-centric urban discourse. It argues that the impacts of neoliberalism on the vulnerable populations – recent immigrants, seniors, and the poor in this case study – vary across the region in complex ways. The geographies of these vulnerable populations in the region have their own specificities that this study explores through the lived materialities of four types of social infrastructure – housing, employment, education, and settlement services. Physical access to these services can reduce or exacerbate vulnerability. In this regard, transportation infrastructure is treated as a mediating factor through its impacts on access to services.

2 York Region, a Prime Example of the Outer Suburbs

This book examines public infrastructure for three vulnerable population groups[1] – recent immigrants, seniors, and the poor – in York Region, a growing outer suburb of the metropolitan Toronto area. York Region is an exemplar of rapid population growth outstripping infrastructural investment. At the time of this study it was the fastest-growing regional municipality within the Greater Toronto Area, and its population growth ranked among the fastest of all suburbs in Canada (CBC 2012). It was also experiencing rapid diversification of its population. Despite the presence of many well-established small towns and villages, most of the development in York Region is low density and oriented towards automobile transportation, with strict separation of residential properties and other land uses. As in many outer suburbs, development in York Region accelerated after 1971 when public spending on all types of infrastructure began to decline. Population growth has occurred without commensurate public investments in human services including public transit. Although the population in York Region is more affluent on average than that in the City of Toronto and in other suburban municipalities in the Toronto metropolitan area such as Peel Region, poverty is growing rapidly in the region. York Region exemplifies the challenges of recent population growth and its diversification in recently developed parts of Canadian metropolitan areas.

---

1 Recent immigrants are people who settled in Canada between 1996 and 2006, seniors are individuals aged sixty-five years and over, and the poor are those whose income falls below the low-income cut-off set by Statistics Canada.

The size of York Region, the third-largest regional municipality in the Toronto metropolitan area, also allows us to explore the infrastructure issues facing three different populations – seniors, recent immigrants, and low-income households. While the three populations overlap, they have distinct infrastructure needs, and each is well represented in York Region (Clarke, Marshall, Ryff, and Rosenthal 2000; Kazemipur and Halli 2000; Lee 2000). These populations are also diverse. As the analysis illustrates later, not all seniors, recent immigrants, or low-income households in York Region are vulnerable and unable to withstand the adverse impacts of various risks to which they are exposed (Cutter 2003). However, we speculate that limited public infrastructure constrains the everyday lives of many from these three groups.

This case study examines social infrastructure, that is, those services and programs that support a safe and healthy community and maintain and promote its quality of life (York Region 2001). It specifically investigates education, employment, housing, and settlement services. Education services include early-childhood education, primary and secondary schooling, post-secondary education, and continuing education for adults. Employment services refer to services that facilitate finding paid employment and establishing self-employment; many employment services target the unemployed and deal with a range of matters such as parental leave, unlawful dismissals, and health and safety issues as well as finding employment. Housing considered in the analysis includes private housing, publicly subsidized social housing units, assisted-living retirement centres, congregate living arrangements, housing information centres, and other housing supports. Settlement services target immigrants by offering language training, orientation classes, individual counselling, and other general information; most clients are adults who have not yet been naturalized as Canadian citizens.

The selection of services in this study was guided by four considerations. First, the services represent the whole range of public infrastructure – from physical infrastructure, such as affordable housing units, to social services, such as public education. Second, the services are the responsibility of all three levels of government, although municipal and provincial governments have the largest roles to play in their provision (Young and Keil 2010). Third, the services are currently of concern to policymakers and planners and to the vulnerable populations themselves (Human Services Planning Coalition York Region 2005). Fourth, recent studies of infrastructure needs in Los Angeles and Europe confirm the importance of these services for social inclusion

(Graham and Marvin 2001; McFarlane and Rutherford 2008; Murie and Musterd 2004; Wolch, Pastor, and Dreier 2004).

The four services were identified through a lengthy process of public consultation, spearheaded by the Human Services Planning Coalition[2] and involving the distribution of nearly fifteen hundred documents to human service providers, representatives of ethno-cultural communities, and members of the public. The consultation included meetings with small groups and a large gathering of over one hundred and eighty participants from ninety-five human service organizations (Catholic Community Services of York Region 2001; Human Services Planning Coalition York Region 2005).

This study recognizes the significance of networked infrastructure for access to services (Graham and Marvin 2001). The use of social services often depends on the availability of transportation infrastructure, particularly the frequency and reliability of public transit and its proximity to major arterial roads. The spatial analysis herein of the distribution of services and vulnerable populations acknowledges that transportation infrastructure is a major facilitator of access to and use of services. Both the availability of public transit and the proximity to arterial roads are considered in the assessments of accessibility for each service being scrutinized.

The Evolving Outer Suburbs

The Regional Municipality of York stretches from the City of Toronto's northern boundary along Steeles Avenue to the southern shore of Lake Simcoe (figure 2.1). Currently, York Region consists of nine diverse local municipalities that include the older towns of Richmond Hill, Aurora, and Newmarket ranged along the north-south axis of Yonge Street and flanked by the municipalities of Vaughan and Markham. Constituting the urbanized part of the regional municipality, these suburban municipalities are fringed by small towns and rural areas – East

---

2 The Human Services Planning Coalition (HSPC) was formed in February 2001 in recognition of the need for long-term, sustainable, integrated planning and funding of human services in York Region. Comprising human service providers and consumers from seventeen sectors, the HSPC represented a pioneering approach to cross-sectoral planning. It was dissolved in 2008. In April 2010 the Human Services Planning Board of York Region was established with the mandate to collaborate on strategies for improving human services in York Region.

Figure 2.1 York Region and its municipalities

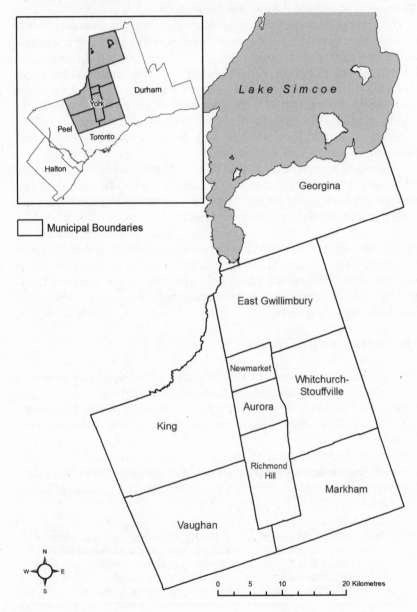

Gwillimbury and Georgina in the north, and King and Whitchurch-Stouffville in the south. Classified as exurban settlements in 1996 by Bunting et al. (2004), the rural part of York Region includes a First Nations settlement in Georgina and one of Canada's wealthiest rural areas in the south-west, King.

With a population of over one million, York Region accounts for 17 per cent of the population in the Toronto metropolitan area. Since the creation of the region in 1971 its population has increased from 169,000 to 1,032,524 in 2011. The region's population expanded by 22.4 per cent between 2001 and 2006, and by 15.7 per cent between 2006 and 2011 (Statistics Canada 2008, 2012b). The largest population increases are concentrated in the southern half of the region, specifically in the City of Vaughan, the Town of Markham,[3] and the Town of Richmond Hill (York Region Planning and Development Services Department 2007).

It is anticipated that by 2031 the region will have 1.5 million residents, and 510,000 households (Council of the Regional Municipality of York 2009, 1). The growth of York Region, and of other suburban regions such as Peel and Durham, is attributable in part to its proximity to the City of Toronto. The supply of new, spacious, single-family detached, and owner-occupied housing has attracted numerous Torontonians. Employment has also increased tenfold, from 49,000 jobs in 1971 to 490,000 in 2008, and the region has attracted more than 29,000 businesses during this period (Council of the Regional Municipality of York 2009). In recent years the growth has included an increase in service-oriented employment and the emergence of a strong knowledge-based economy, more so than in Peel Region, the largest suburban region of Toronto. With its expanding supply of new housing and increasing job opportunities, York Region has become a major growth area in the Toronto metropolitan area (York Region Planning and Development Services Department 2008).

Population growth has been accompanied by increasing social diversity. According to the 2006 census, the immigrant population made up 43 per cent of the region's population (Statistics Canada 2008), and English was the mother tongue for about 61 per cent of the region's population. The ethnic and racial backgrounds of the population are diverse. In 2006, Markham was the only municipality in the Toronto

---

3 On 1 July 2012 the Town of Markham became the City of Markham.

metropolitan area in which the majority of the population identified themselves as a visible minority.

Overall, the region is affluent. In 2005 about 44 per cent of its residents had an average annual income of more than $70,000. However, poverty is a growing social issue. In 2005, 12.7 per cent of the population had an annual income that was below the low-income cut-off. The median income for a poor individual was $8,846, about one-third of the regional median. When multiple earners in a household are considered, incomes still vary tremendously across the region. In 2005 the median household income ranged from $91,762 in King Township to $65,645 in Georgina.

The population is aging, and the number of seniors is growing rapidly. People who were sixty-five years of age and over accounted for 9.9 per cent of the population in 2006. York Region's reputation as a bedroom community for young families is no longer true, if it ever was.

A History of Diversity

The earliest human settlement in the area now known as York Region began at the end of the Wisconsin glaciation approximately nine thousand years ago. Palaeo-Indians lived for millennia as a hunting and gathering society of largely nomadic bands. About a thousand years ago agriculture became important, and by 1500 AD, the Late Iroquoian period, several Aboriginal societies in the region had a strong dependence on agriculture, alongside a regional political system of alliances and confederacies.[4]

In the late 1780s the Crown bought the area around Toronto (from the Humber River to the Don River), and the Carrying Place Route, the traditional route up the Humber River through Lake Simcoe to Georgian Bay. As part of the effort to attract settlers, many military officials and Americans from Pennsylvania and New York were granted land in the area in return for their loyalty and service during the war of 1812. In the early 1800s, York County stretched from Lake Ontario to north of Lake Simcoe and was divided into York (Toronto), Vaughan, Markham, King, East Gwillimbury, Whitchurch, North Gwillimbury, and Georgina,

---

4 This section draws primarily from discussions in Byers, Kennedy, McBurney, and Robertson (1976), sources listed in http://www.rootsweb.ancestry.com/~onyork/research-books.html, and websites pertaining to each municipality in the region.

along with much of what is now Peel and Durham regions and the County of Simcoe. Newmarket, Richmond Hill, and Aurora were created later as municipal units from the respective townships to the east and west of Yonge Street. North Gwillimbury was amalgamated with Georgina as residential patterns changed over the years. The Township of Georgina is home to the only Native reserve in the region, that of the Chippewas of Georgina Island, whose reserve includes Snake and Fox islands.

In 1954 Metropolitan Toronto was established, creating a regional urban government that was severed from its rural hinterland in the rest of York County (Frisken 2007; Sewell 2009). Growth and development continued in the southern part of York County while the northern half of the region remained rural. In response to development pressures the six southern municipalities and townships created an informal committee to deal with planning issues, but each municipality was free to act independently, as was the county government. The interests of the York County government and the southern municipalities and townships differed, particularly regarding governance issues. While York County lobbied to become the senior level of municipal government akin to Metropolitan Toronto, Richmond Hill asked the Province of Ontario to sever from the county the five southern municipalities that were experiencing rapid urbanization (Sewell 2009). In 1970 the Ontario government responded by passing Bill 102, which amalgamated the townships and villages of York County into the nine municipalities that exist today. A regional government representing a second tier of municipal governance was introduced in January 1971. Despite the tensions between York County and the southern municipalities, the imposition of a regional government was quite well received by local municipalities. The long history of collaboration, albeit informal, among the southern municipalities, and the county's interest in becoming a regional government, ensured that York Region avoided many of the disputes that occurred in surrounding regions such as Peel (Sewell 2009).

The regional government was intended to reduce competition for development and the assessments that result, create economies of scale for the provision of specific municipal services, and set a strong foundation for future growth (Frisken 2007; Sewell 2009). The regional government would be responsible for the expensive physical infrastructure such as transportation, transit, water, and waste water that shapes the location and pace of urban development. According to Sewell (2009), regional government in general was promoted by the Province because it allowed for the logical location of industry within a region while ensuring that all parts of the region benefited from the resulting increases in property taxes. Policing, social housing, emergency services, licensing of childcare, and administration of social assistance were also under the purview of the regional municipality. Land-use planning, parks and recreational services, and by-law enforcement are some of the main responsibilities of the local municipalities.

The two tiers of local government are closely intertwined (Frisken 2007). Mayors from local municipalities sit on the regional council and appoint the chief executive officer. Nevertheless, policy and program differences sometimes emerge between the two levels of government. For example, transportation policy has been a cause of tension in the past decade. The recent dispute about road expansion revealed the continuing division in York Region between the dense, urbanized municipalities in the southern half of the region and the rural, northern municipalities that are seeking development (Grech 2008).[5] At the same time, the two-tier system of municipal government reduces political pressures on elected municipal officials. Major costs such as social housing and transportation are borne by the regional government, while councillors in local municipalities can boast of zero tax increases for local municipalities. Appreciating the political benefits of a two-tier system, the majority of councillors in local municipalities recently opposed proposals for officials to be elected directly to the regional level of government.[6]

Existing Infrastructure

York Region is undergoing rapid demographic, social, and economic change. Its population is diverse, as is the infrastructure that is available to serve it. A description of the existing infrastructure provides the context for appreciating the issues associated with the emerging geographies of vulnerability and accessibility.

---

5 According to the regional transportation plan, wider roads are needed to deal with congestion, particularly in the southern half of the region. After lengthy environmental assessments and community consultations, councillors in the Town of Markham passed a resolution opposing street widening, a move that has delayed implementation of much of the region's transportation plan (Grech 2008).

6 In 2012, Social Planning York Region held public meetings to garner support for a private member's bill in the Ontario legislature that called for direct election of a chair of York Region Council instead of the the appointment of a chief executive officer.

Transportation

Like many suburbs, York Region has a transportation system that is oriented to the use of automobiles (Miller and Shalaby 2004; OECD 2010). Despite recent large investments in public transit, the automobile remains the predominant mode of transportation. In 2006, 86 per cent of all trips made by residents of York Region were made in an automobile, mainly by drivers (Data Management Group 2009). On a weekday, only 6 per cent of all trips were made by transit. Transit is used more often for the journey to work, accounting for 10 per cent of all trips made between 6:00 a.m. and 9:00 a.m. The reliance on the automobile has persisted despite small decreases in the average trip length, from 8.1 kilometres in 1986 to 6.1 kilometres in 2006 (Data Management Group 2009).

The automobile dependency of the region reflects the paucity of transit service. A rush-hour commuter rail service (GO Transit) that connects the region to downtown Toronto is operated by Metrolinx, a provincially funded transportation agency that is charged with developing and promoting sustainable transportation across the entire Toronto metropolitan area and beyond. Buses are the main mode of public transportation within the region. In addition to GO buses that cross regional boundaries under the auspices of Metrolinx, York Region operates its own bus system that consists of Viva and York Regional Transit (YRT).

Viva, the region's initial foray into rapid transit, is a bus system that connects the five large urban municipalities in York Region – Markham, Richmond Hill, Vaughan, Aurora, and Newmarket – with each other and with the Toronto subway system, GO Transit, and the Region of Peel. It operates along major corridors much like an above-ground subway, making infrequent stops. The buses are equipped with a Global Positioning System (GPS) that allows drivers to control traffic lights. At the time of writing, dedicated lanes were under construction on selected sections of the Viva network to increase its speed and reliability.

The YRT is a local bus service that connects all nine municipalities of York Region and feeds into the Viva network. With more than one hundred routes including conventional services, GO shuttles, express services, community buses, and high-school, college, and university services, the YRT was developed by amalgamating bus systems that were operated originally by individual municipalities. As a result, the YRT has its densest and most frequent service in the southern half of the region, where the population has historically been concentrated (figure 2.2).

Figure 2.2 York Region bus routes, 2006

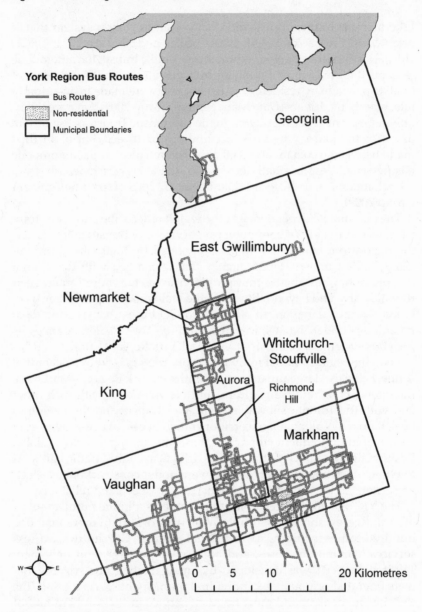

Source: York Region Department of Geomatics (2006)

Although service is often less frequent and the network is sparser than in the City of Toronto, Viva and the YRT provide better service than do transit systems in the Peel and Durham regions, the two regional municipalities neighbouring York Region. In Peel Region the two largest municipalities, Mississauga and Brampton, operate independent bus systems with separate schedules and networks. In Durham Region the network for the regional bus service remains sparse.

Rapid population and employment growth in York Region has exacerbated congestion. Despite the recent investments in public transit, travel is slow during peak hours (Miller and Shalaby 2004). Congestion increases travel times by 59 per cent on average (Greater Toronto Transportation Authority 2008), so that a trip that would normally take twenty minutes now takes more than thirty minutes. Residents are acutely aware of congestion and usually raise the issue at public meetings held to discuss proposed land developments (Gombu 2010). Employers share residents' concerns. In recent surveys (Polonsky 2011; York Region 2004), they emphasized the urgency of dealing with congestion. They noted that congestion not only increases commuting times and adds to commuting costs but also makes it difficult for employers to hire workers from northern locations in the region where transit service is infrequent (York Region 2004).

Housing

Housing in York Region is typical of the outer suburbs (Bunting et al. 2004; Suttor 2007) with a preponderance of private-market housing that individuals rent or own, paying what the market will bear at the time of the rental agreement or the dwelling purchase. The supply of social housing – subsidized rental housing for people with low to moderate incomes, seniors, or people with special needs – is limited. Public housing that is owned and operated by municipalities predominates. There is some cooperative housing, in which the residents manage the housing development, and some non-profit housing owned and managed by non-profit groups such as religious organizations and ethnic communities. Some assisted living facilities, retirement residences, and congregate living arrangements are also available in York Region, but they are in short supply and have long waiting lists. There are also two housing information centres that offer support.

The majority of the region's housing stock is single-family, detached housing that is owner occupied. In 2006, private rental units made up only 11.7 per cent of the housing stock in the region (Statistics Canada 2006). Of a total of 275,200 households, only 32,255 were living in rental accommodation. Housing tenure in York Region is typical of outer suburbs, where the supply of rental accommodation has always been limited (Bunting et al. 2004; Suttor 2007). The absence of rental housing is associated with the dominance of single-family, detached housing units that make up 72 per cent of the housing stock, the highest percentage in any of the regional municipalities of the Toronto metropolitan area. Apartments represented only 12 per cent of the housing stock (York Region 2007), a much smaller proportion than in the other regional municipalities that comprise the Toronto metropolitan area.[7]

Social housing is in short supply, with only 6,385 units of public housing owned and managed by the regional municipality in 2006 and another 4,482 units of subsidized non-profit and cooperative housing. Several faith and ethnic communities spearheaded the development of non-profit and cooperative housing; however, at the time of this case study, none of this housing targeted a specific ethno-racial group.[8] People gain access to social housing through a waiting list, which was estimated to include 5,490 households in 2006. This number grew to 5,838 households in 2008. Only women with children who are victims of domestic violence have special priority on the waiting list (Turner 2008). Social housing developments vary in size, but at the time of this study there were eighty-three different developments in York Region.[9]

In addition to social housing, there are a limited number of assisted-living housing units in York Region that provide supportive housing and group living. Nineteen retirement residences and thirty-two congregate living arrangements, long-term-care facilities, domiciliary hostels, special-care homes, and group homes serve seniors and low-income residents. Although eligibility for social housing is based largely on income, other criteria, such as health status, are relevant for the assisted

---

7 For example, in 2006 apartments comprised 23 per cent and 16 per cent of the housing stock in Peel Region and Durham Region, respectively. In the City of Toronto, apartments were the dominant type of dwelling, accounting for more than half of the housing stock (Statistics Canada 2006).

8 The policy changed in 2009 when the Regional Municipality of York agreed that non-profit-housing providers could discriminate among applicants on the basis of ethnic identity and religion.

9 Social housing has been funded by the municipal governments since the Province of Ontario downloaded responsibility for social housing in the last half of the 1990s (Hackworth and Moriah 2006).

and congregate living facilities. In many instances, residents of assisted-living developments must either pay market rents or receive housing subsidies. Housing information and counselling about how to obtain and keep housing are also available at thirteen locations in the region.

York Region has higher housing costs than those of many other parts of the Toronto metropolitan area. The average sales price of a single-family detached dwelling in June 2005 was $477,000. By comparison, in Peel and Durham regions, the average sales prices for an equivalent house were $418,000 and $297,000, respectively. Only in Halton Region and the City of Toronto did the average sales prices exceed that in York Region (York Region 2007).

High sales prices translate into high rents and large monthly payments for owners in York Region. In 2005 the average gross monthly rent in York Region was $1,042, compared with an average of $874 in Durham Region and $931 in the City of Toronto (Statistics Canada 2006). Although there was less variation in the average major payments paid by homeowners, York Region had the highest average monthly major payment ($1,490) in the Toronto census metropolitan area. In comparison, the equivalent monthly payment for mortgage, utilities, and taxes in the City of Toronto was $1,312 (Statistics Canada 2006).

Employment Patterns

Jobs are concentrated in the southern part of York Region, specifically in Vaughan, Markham, and Richmond Hill, which together accounted for almost 80 per cent of jobs in the region in 2006. Newmarket, where the regional government is located, is a fourth employment node, with 42,100 jobs or 9 per cent of the regional total. In 2009 manufacturing remained the largest employment sector, accounting for 17 per cent of total employment (75,300 jobs). It was followed closely by personal services and business services, each representing about 16 per cent of total employment or about 70,000 jobs.

With 493,000 jobs in 2009, York Region is a growing employment node within the Toronto metropolitan area (Boudreau, Keil, and Young 2009; Miller and Shalaby 2004; Turcotte and Ruel 2008). York Region's share of employment in the metropolitan area increased from 8 per cent in 1986 to 15 per cent in 2006. Employment growth has exacerbated traffic congestion. In York Region the jobs are much more dispersed than in the centre of Toronto (Miller and Shalaby 2004), and long work trips are increasingly the norm (Data Management Group 2009).

The industrial mix in York Region is shifting from goods production to services. Since 1998, health care and social assistance, F.I.R.E. (finance, insurance, and real estate), and business services all increased their employment totals by more than 80 per cent (York Region 2009). At the same time, manufacturing employment declined from 26 per cent of all jobs in 1998 to 17 per cent in 2009. Some of the employment growth stems from population growth. For example, between 1998 and 2009, health care and social services increased by 88 per cent, public administration by 84 per cent, and retail trade by 65 per cent, largely as a result of increasing population (York Region 2009).

The industrial mix is also shifting in the Toronto CMA. Manufacturing remains the largest employer in the metropolitan area, where it accounted for 11.5 per cent of all employment in 2010. However, the metropolitan economy lost approximately 11,000 manufacturing jobs annually throughout the decade. By 2010, manufacturing accounted for a smaller percentage of total employment in the Toronto CMA than in York Region (York Region 2010). Jobs are increasing in the second- and third-largest sectors in the metropolitan area: the professional, scientific, and technical services sector and the retail trade sector, each of which accounts for approximately 11 per cent of employment or 320,000 jobs. The fastest-growing sectors include health care and social assistance; finance, insurance and real estate; and education, with each sector having 258,000 to 208,000 jobs.

Social Services

Although a wide range of social services is offered by numerous public and non-profit agencies in York Region, per capita funding continues to lag behind the provincial and metropolitan averages. Social services have scrambled to expand as the regional population has increased and vulnerable groups have grown rapidly. The challenges of growth have been intensified by funding changes at all levels of government over the past two decades. While the federal government represents the largest share of social services spending, the relative importance of this spending has declined significantly. Federal government spending on social services accounted for 49 per cent of expenditures in 2007, compared with 59 per cent in 1989 (*The Daily* 2007). Until 2007 the picture in Ontario was one of declining provincial spending as well; overall, total social program expenditures declined from 18.1 per cent in 1989 to 14.8 per cent in 2007.

In this context, social service funding in Ontario suburbs has proved to be an ongoing problem. A report by PricewaterhouseCoopers LLP (2006) for the Strong Communities Coalition (a coalition of Toronto's four surrounding regional municipalities: Durham, Halton, Peel, and York) found a sizeable gap between the per capita annual operating funding for social services in the coalition and that in the rest of Ontario. The report also found that the annual operating funding gap had grown by 33.8 per cent in total funding and by 18 per cent in per capita funding between 2002–3 and 2006–7. For example, Peel Region has 8.7 per cent of Ontario's population but receives only 4.4 per cent of the Province's social service funding (Funston 2005). In a similar manner, in 2000–1, per capita funding for settlement services in York Region was $299.83, significantly less than Toronto's per capita amount of $680.13 and the rest of the Greater Toronto Area's per capita average of $659.98.

With the downloading of responsibility for several social services from the provincial to the municipal governments, the provincial government also mandated pooling arrangements in which York Region and other regional governments in the metropolitan area contributed to the costs of social housing and social assistance in the City of Toronto (Boudreau, Keil, and Young 2009). When pooling ended in 2013, York Region had paid more than $1 billion. Annual savings for the region are estimated to be over $100 million per year thereafter. For York Region politicians and residents, the end of pooling provides a welcome opportunity to reinvest locally in social services.

As a consequence of a funding approach that has not responded to the major suburban growth spurt of the last two decades, per capita spending on services for both adults and children has not increased proportionately (Pembina Institute 2007), and provincial initiatives in these areas have tended to be both narrowly focused and time limited; thus, they have not yielded ongoing and predictable resources for service providers (York Region Human Services Planning Coalition 2003). Spending on social services within York Region is estimated to total $77.6 billion for 2001–26. If this amount were increased to bring it to the provincial per capita average and keep pace with inflation, an aging population, and capital needs, it would total $120.9 billion (York Region 2001).

The Metropolitan Context

York Region stands out as a rapidly growing part of the Toronto metropolitan area. Between 2001 and 2006 the population of York Region alone grew by 22.4 per cent, more than double the increase in the total metropolitan population (9.2 per cent) (table 2.1). With rapid growth, the population in York Region is more diverse and now shares many characteristics of the metropolitan population. Although their absolute numbers are smaller in York Region than in the Toronto CMA, seniors and immigrants now account for similar percentages of the total population in each location. Population growth in York Region is fuelled more by the suburbanization of successful and well-established immigrants than by the direct settlement of recently arrived newcomers. In 2006 only 12.3 per cent of the York Region population had immigrated within the past ten years, far less than the 16.0 per cent of the total metropolitan population. York Region continues to be more affluent than the Toronto CMA as a whole, even though the number of low-income households has increased steadily in the past two decades. In 2006 approximately one in eight York Region residents, 12.7 per cent, reported an income that was less than the low-income cut-off. The per cent of low-income persons is still lower in York Region than in the Toronto metropolitan area, where 18.4 per cent of the population reported an income that was below the low-income cut-off.

As expected, the housing stock in York Region is newer than that in the City of Toronto, with an emphasis on low-rise, owner-occupied properties and a concomitant absence of apartments and rental units. Almost two-thirds of the York Region housing stock, 62.6 per cent, was constructed after 1985, close to double the percentage in the Toronto CMA (34.9 per cent) (table 2.1). Most housing in the region, 84.2 per cent, comprises single-family detached, semi-detached, and row houses. The predominance of low-rise dwelling units contrasts with the relatively equal split between low-rise and high-rise units in the metropolitan area (table 2.1). The emphasis on low-rise housing is evident in the high percentage of owner-occupied units in York Region, 88.3 per cent. versus 67.6 per cent in the Toronto CMA.

In terms of educational attainment and labour-force participation, York Region is representative of the Toronto CMA. Almost a third of adults have a university certificate, degree, or diploma, and approximately half have a non-university certificate or diploma. High levels of educational attainment are associated with high rates of labour-force participation and low unemployment rates. In 2006 both trends were evident in York Region where labour-market statistics indicate that the York Region population aged fifteen and over is slightly more likely to participate in the labour force and slightly less likely to be unemployed than the equivalent metropolitan population (table 2.1). As a result of

Table 2.1 Selected population and dwelling characteristics in York Region and the Toronto census metropolitan area (CMA), 2006

	Toronto CMA	York Region
Total population in 2006	5,113,149	892,712
Population change from 2001	9.2%	22.4%
Seniors (65 years and over)	11.9%	10.3%
Immigrants	45.7%	42.9%
Recent (1996–2006) immigrants	16.0%	12.3%
Low-incomes	18.4%	12.7%
Total private dwellings	1,801,255	275,680
Constructed after 1985	34.9%	62.6%
Detached, semi-detached, and row houses	57.7%	84.2%
Owned	67.6%	88.3%
Population aged 15 and over	4,122,820	709,550
With no educational certificate, diploma, or degree	19.7%	19.0%
With non-university certificates or diploma	47.9%	48.7%
With university certificate, diploma, or degree	32.4%	32.4%
Labour-force participation rate	68.3%	70.5%
Unemployment rate	6.7%	5.4%
Median income	$26,754	$28,829
Total experienced labour force aged 15 and over, employed in:	2,758,700	492,530
Agriculture and other resource-based industries	1.1%	1.3%
Construction	5.4%	6.6%
Manufacturing	13.5%	13.3%
Wholesale trade	6.0%	6.7%
Retail trade	10.6%	11.6%
Finance and real estate	9.4%	9.7%
Health care and social services	8.1%	7.5%
Educational services	6.3%	6.8%
Business services	23.9%	21.1%
Other services	15.8%	15.4%
Total private households	1,801,245	275,680
Median household income	$69,321	$81,872
Owners spending 30% or more monthly on housing	26.4%	27.3%
Renters spending 30% or more monthly on housing	46.3%	48.0%
Average monthly owner payment	$1,405	$1,490
Average monthly rent	$970	$1,402

Source: Statistics Canada, 2006 Census of Population

the similarity in labour-market participation, median personal income is only slightly higher in York Region than in the Toronto CMA, $28,829 compared with $26,754.

The parallels between the labour markets in York Region and those in the metropolitan area are evident when one compares the industries in which the experienced labour force at each location is employed. Business services, other services, manufacturing, and retail trade are the four biggest employers of residents from York Region and the Toronto CMA. The data in table 2.1 describe the industries in which residents are employed, not the locations of their workplaces. A separate analysis of workplaces suggests that manufacturing accounts for a larger share of all jobs in York Region than in the Toronto CMA (York Region 2010). The disparities between the industries of workplaces in York Region and the industries in which residents are employed are indicative of the high commuting volumes in the region. A 2006 transportation survey indicated that approximately half of the York Region labour force came from within the region and the remainder travelled daily to York Region, mainly from the City of Toronto and Peel Region (Data Management Group 2009).

At the household level the residents of York Region are markedly more affluent than the metropolitan population as a whole. The median household income for the Toronto CMA was $69,321 in 2006, much less than the median household income of $81,872 in York Region. Despite the high household incomes in York Region, households in both locations are equally likely to be experiencing financial stress as a result of the disparity between household income and housing costs. Approximately one-quarter of owners and almost half of renters in the region and in the metropolitan area spend at least 30 per cent of their total income on housing (table 2.1). Although the average monthly costs for homeowners in York Region are similar to those in the entire metropolitan area, rents in York Region are substantially higher than in the metropolitan area. Indeed, York Region renters are paying almost 50 per cent more than renters in the entire CMA.

A comparison of York Region with the Toronto metropolitan area underscores the complexity of the outer suburbs. Despite its affluence at the household level, rapid population growth is associated with the emergence of vulnerable populations. The percentages of the population that are recent immigrants and that have low incomes are growing but remain lower than in the metropolitan area. On the one hand, labour-market conditions as described by rates of labour-force participation and unemployment and by personal incomes largely mirror those in the entire metropolitan area. On the other hand, the housing stock stands out as stereotypically suburban with a marked emphasis on low-rise, owner-occupied dwellings. For renters, the shortage of apartments translates into high rents, well above the metropolitan average.

Emerging Geographies

This book describes and analyses the geographies of vulnerability in York Region by identifying the residential patterns of recent immigrants, seniors, and low-income households and examining the availability of education, employment, housing, and settlement services in the region. Access by the three vulnerable groups to these four social services, as well as their awareness of, use of, and satisfaction with these services, is considered. Like previous Canadian studies that have focused on settlement patterns and relied on the analysis of secondary data (for example, Bourne et al. 2003; Bunting, Filion, and Walks 2004; Suttor 2007; Taylor 2011; Young and Keil 2010), this study draws upon information from the 2006 census[10] and an inventory of service providers to identify disparities in service provision for the three vulnerable groups. The analysis of secondary data is complemented by the collection of primary data concerning each group's awareness of, use of, and satisfaction with education, employment, housing, and settlement services in the region. The detailed analysis of information from a survey provides insight into different residents' opinions about the availability of services and their experiences with them. This research is innovative in its use of geographic information systems (GIS) to compare the proximity of services across the three vulnerable groups. The primary data collected for this study add to the understanding of the suburbs that has been gained from earlier research which relied on secondary data from the census, municipal planning documents, and media.

The goal is to situate the case study of York Region in current debates about the changing nature of suburbs. Chapter 1 has set out the context for this case study by reviewing the recent literature concerning the links between vulnerability and neoliberalism in the suburbs and

---

10 The research for this study was conducted prior to the 2011 census. Our preparation would have benefited from an update of the census data had the 2011 Canadian census been conducted in the same manner as in previous years. In 2011, replacement of the compulsory long-form census by a voluntary national household survey renders data reliability questionable.

justifying our choice of York Region. In what follows, chapter 3 will profile recent immigrants, seniors, and people with low incomes in York Region; chapters 4 to 7 will examine, for all vulnerable population groups, their access to, awareness of, use of, and satisfaction with a particular human service, starting with education services and followed by employment, housing, and settlement services; and chapter 8 will use the findings concerning service provision for the three vulnerable population groups to comment on the impacts of neoliberalism in the outer suburbs.

3 Vulnerability in York Region

Patterns and Trends

Increasing social diversity and growing vulnerability characterize York Region. In 2006, immigrants made up 43 per cent of the region's population, and recent immigrants (those arriving within the last ten years of the census) rose by two-and-a-half times, from 40,875 in 1991 to 109,275 in 2006 (Statistics Canada 2008). The population is also aging rapidly. In 1991 there were 35,560 seniors in the region. By 2011, their number had reached 120,936. Growing income disparities are apparent. In 1991, 37,570 individuals lived in households with incomes less than the low-income cut-off.[1] By 2006 the figure was 112,165. These growth trends are illustrated in figure 3.1.

The proportions of recent immigrants, seniors, and low-income people in suburban York Region and the central City of Toronto in 2001 and 2006 are compared. While these proportions were higher in the City of Toronto in each census year, the rates of increase in these populations were higher in York Region. For example, the senior population in York Region increased by 37.4 per cent from 63,790 in 2001 to 87,620

---

1 Low-income cut-offs (LICOs) are income thresholds (determined by analysing family expenditure data) below which families will devote a larger share of income to the necessities of food, shelter, and clothing than would the average family. To reflect differences in the costs of necessities among different community and family sizes, LICOs are defined for five categories of community size and seven categories of family size (Statistics Canada 2005a). For York Region they range from $20,778 for a one-person family to $54,987 for families with over seven people.

Figure 3.1   Growth of vulnerable populations in York Region, 1981–2006

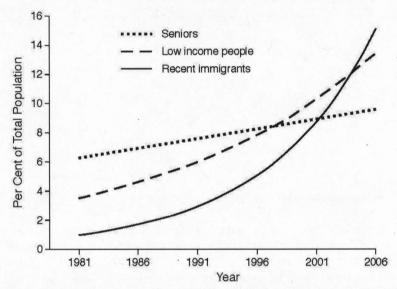

Note: In 1981, recent immigrants refer to those arriving in Canada three years before the census; in 1991, 2001, and 2006 the period of arrival is ten years.

Sources: Statistics Canada 1981 and 1991 Census Profile Data; Statistics Canada 2006, 2007a, 2008

in 2006, but in the City of Toronto the increase was only 4.5 per cent from 319,405 in 2001 to 333,730 in 2006. As a proportion of the total population, seniors increased by 1.1 per cent (8.8 per cent in 2001 and 9.9 per cent in 2006) in York Region, and only 0.4 per cent (12.9 per cent in 2001 and 13.3 per cent in 2006) in the City of Toronto.

In York Region, social vulnerability is not only growing but also spreading. Figures 3.2 to 3.4 detail the spatial distributions of seniors, recent immigrants, and low-income people between 1981 and 2006. The spatial patterns of seniors in York Region reflect a population that is aging in place. On average the number of seniors increased between 1981 and 2006. In 1981 no census tract had more than 1,140 seniors, and only two census tracts had more than 800 seniors. By 2006 there were twenty-four census tracts in which 801 to 1,960 seniors lived (figure 3.2). As many people age in place, seniors now live throughout York Region. The belt of census tracts in the middle of the region where seniors were

Figure 3.2 Distribution of seniors by census tract in York Region, 1981–2006

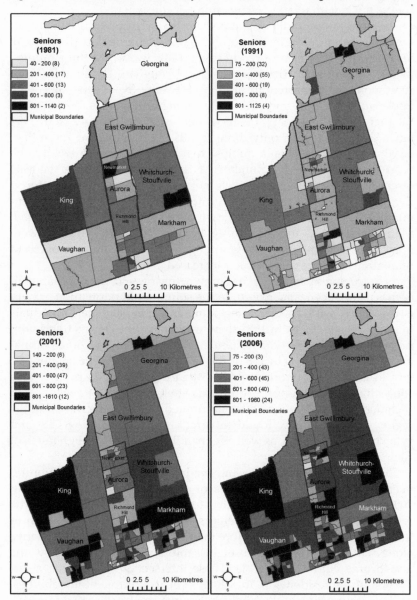

Source: Statistics Canada 1983, 1993, 2003, 2008

most numerous in 1981 has shattered. In all parts of the region there are census tracts with relatively large numbers of seniors.

The recent immigrant population has also increased substantially but remains concentrated in the southern half of the region (figure 3.3). Specifically, 92 per cent of recent immigrants live in the three munici-palities of Markham, Richmond Hill, and Vaughan. The southern con-centration has persisted for the past twenty-five years. Since the information for 1981 indicates only immigrants who had arrived in the preceding three years, the focus here is on the changes from 1991 onwards. In that year, only three census tracts contained more than 1,500 recent immigrants, a number that had increased to twenty-one census tracts by 2006. The numbers of census tracts with more than 900 recent immigrants increased even more, from fifteen in 1991 to forty-five in 2006. As these numbers indicate, the concentration of recent im-migrants in the southern part of the region has expanded and intensified. More census tracts in Vaughan, Richmond Hill, and Markham were home to large numbers of recent immigrants, and the number of recent immigrants in these census tracts increased.

As the region's population has grown, the low-income population in each census tract has increased. In the south, rapid population growth is associated with an increasing number of low-income individuals in many census tracts. In 1981 there were only nine census tracts with more than 250 low-income residents. By 2006 the low-income popula-tion had exceeded 250 in 136 of the 154 census tracts. The spatial pat-tern in 2006 is also more dispersed than in 1981, when poverty was concentrated along a north-south axis stretching from Newmarket to Richmond Hill. Although still concentrated in the southern half of the region, poverty is now found in rural areas such as King City and Whitchurch-Stouffville, as well as expanding steadily through much of Georgina in the north.

The spatial patterns of low-income individuals in York Region re-flect the overlapping dimensions of vulnerability. For example, in 2006, recent immigrants accounted for more than one-quarter of the low-income population, and seniors comprised almost one-tenth of the low-income population. More than one in four recent immigrants, along with more than one in eight seniors, had incomes below the low-income cut-off (table 3.1). These intersections show that a fair portion of the residents of York Region bear multiple vulnerabilities. Those with multiple vulnerabilities are in even greater need of acces-sible services.

Figure 3.3   Distribution of recent immigrants by census tract in York Region, 1981–2006

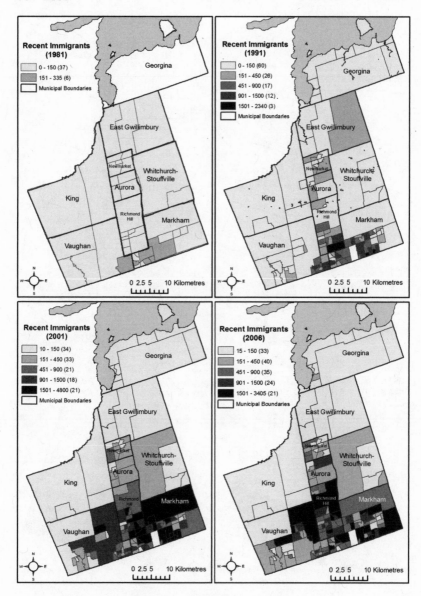

Source: Statistics Canada 1983, 1993, 2003, 2008

Figure 3.4 Distribution of low-income individuals by census tract in York Region, 1981–2006

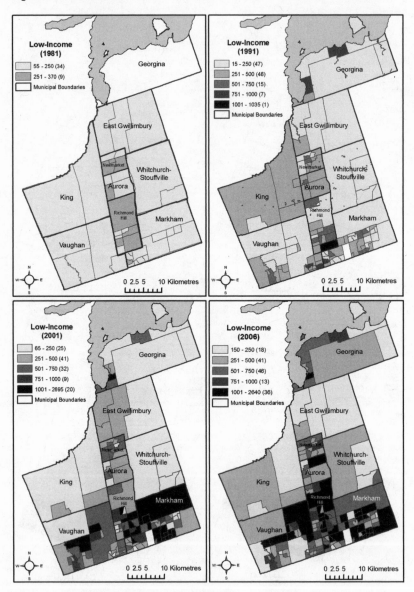

Source: Statistics Canada 1983, 1993, 2003, 2008

Table 3.1   Population size of vulnerable groups, 2006

	Recent immigrants		Low-income		Seniors	
	N.	%	N	%	N	%
Recent immigrants	109,275	100.0	29,580	26.4	7,065	8.1
Low-income	29,580	27.1	112,165	100.0	10,700	12.2
Seniors	7,065	6.5	10,700	9.5	87,620	100.0

Source: Statistics Canada 2008, calculations by authors

Figure 3.5 identifies areas of multiple vulnerabilities, that is, areas that are above the regional median in terms of two or three dimensions.[2] For example, the numbers of recent immigrants and of low-income residents often exceed the medians in these census tracts, or the numbers of seniors and low-income residents are above the median. In census tracts with triple vulnerability, the numbers of all three populations are higher than the regional median. As figure 3.5 illustrates, areas of multiple vulnerabilities are concentrated in Markham and Richmond Hill, the municipalities in which rapid population growth is attributed to the arrival of numerous recent immigrants and there are growing numbers of seniors. Both social groups are disproportionately represented in the low-income population. The employment and income challenges facing recent immigrants who struggle to have their credentials and experience recognized are well documented (Picot 2008), while retirement is associated with low income for many seniors (Townson 2006). Unlike those in the City of Toronto, the areas of multiple vulnerabilities are within some of the most affluent neighbourhoods in the metropolitan area and in urban Canada. Visibly, they are well-groomed, single-family homes among the many culs-de-sac in the outer suburb.

The geography of vulnerability is uneven. The magnitude is stronger in the southern part of the York Region, which, being closer to

---

2 The map in figure 3.5 bears strong resemblance to a map showing social deprivation in the region, where social deprivation is represented by a composite index measuring fourteen attributes: recent immigrants, visible minorities, people with no official language capability, people with only primary education, part-time workers, unskilled workers, unemployed individuals, seniors, seniors living alone, renters, persons in single-parent households, people with low income, people with no income, and income distance from the regional average.

Figure 3.5 Vulnerable neighbourhoods in York Region, 2006

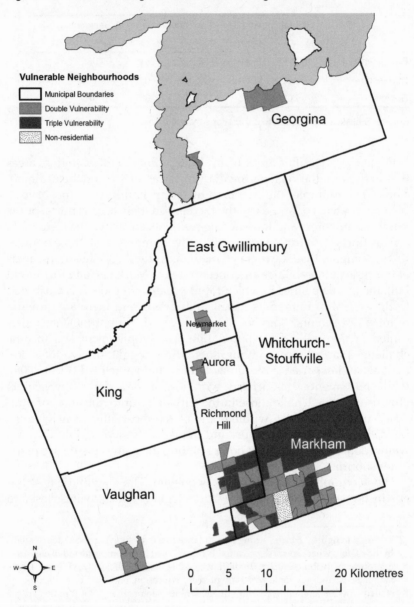

Source: Statistics Canada 2008

Toronto, is more urbanized and more populous. However, vulnerability is found in all parts of the region. The different spatial patterns for each dimension of vulnerability and for the areas of multiple vulnerabilities underscore the diversity of the outer suburbs. Vulnerability also takes different forms in different parts of York Region. The remainder of this study argues that vulnerability is subject to different social processes in the northern and southern parts of York Region. The hypothesis is that the low-income populations in the north are largely seniors with low incomes, whereas low incomes in the south are primarily caused by the concentration of recent immigrants, who find it difficult to enter the labour market at a level commensurate with their credentials. In the south there are also areas of multiple vulnerabilities where recent immigrants struggling with low incomes live close to low-income seniors, and thus both processes of marginalization are at work.

Recent Immigrants

For census purposes, Statistics Canada defines recent immigrants as those who have lived in Canada for less than five years at the time of the census. In this book the definition of recent immigrants is extended to include those who had been in Canada for less than ten years at the time of the 2006 census (that is, those who landed in Canada after 1995) because many studies show that, with significant changes in the composition of Canada's immigrants in the last two decades, the settlement process takes much longer than it did before.

According to the definition used in this study, in 2006, 109,270 recent immigrants resided in York Region, accounting for 12.3 per cent of the region's total population (table 3.2). Their demographic and social attributes suggest mixed implications with respect to their need for settlement services. Forty-three per cent of them had lived in Canada for less than five years, and the other 57 per cent for five to ten years. Fifty-seven per cent of all the recent immigrants were in their prime years (25–54 years of age) for active participation in the labour force. This is 12 per cent higher than the total population. Accordingly, their share of seniors was smaller, 6.5 per cent versus 9.9 per cent in the total population. They were also well educated, with 40 per cent of those who were fifteen years of age and older possessing university credentials (compared with only 26 per cent for the total population). It is unclear, though, how much of this human capital was obtained in Canada

Table 3.2 Attributes of recent immigrants in York Region, 2006

	Total population		Total recent immigrants		Recent immigrants as % of total population
	N	%	n	%	(n/N)
Population	886,575	100.0	109,270	100.0	12.3
0–14 years old	177,675	20.0	15,145	13.9	8.5
15–24 years old	126,240	14.2	18,130	16.6	14.4
25–34 years old	107,325	12.1	19,335	17.7	18.0
35–44 years old	150,880	17.0	26,360	24.1	17.5
45–54 years old	143,385	16.2	16,625	15.2	11.6
55–64 years old	93,445	10.5	6,605	6.0	7.1
65 years old and over	87,620	9.9	7,065	6.5	8.1
By period of immigration:					
Immigrant population	380,375	42.9	109,270	100.0	28.7
1996–2001	130,185	34.2	62,835	57.5	48.3
2001–2006	46,435	12.2	46,435	42.5	100.0
By education level:					
Population aged 15 years and over	708,895	80.0	94,125	86.1	13.3
No certificate, diploma, or degree	134,325	18.9	15,275	16.2	11.4
High-school graduation certificate, or equivalent certificate	181,335	25.6	20,580	21.9	11.3
Apprenticeship or trades certificate, or diploma, certificate, or diploma below the bachelor level	206,000	29.1	20,970	22.3	10.2
University certificate, diploma, or degree	187,230	26.4	37,300	39.6	19.9

Source: Statistics Canada 2008

where recognition of foreign education credentials has been a concern expressed by many Canadian employers.

Not surprisingly, the unemployment rate was 2 per cent higher for recent immigrants than for the total population in York Region (7.5 per cent versus 5.4 per cent). While 60.3 per cent of the York Region population worked full time, fewer recent immigrants worked full time, and disproportionately more were engaged in part-time work (52.6 per cent). Also, while equal proportions of the total population and the recent immigrant population (34.0 per cent) were employed in upper-skill-level occupations, larger proportions of recent immigrants (23.3 per cent) were engaged in lower-skilled occupations such as sales and service and manual labour compared with their more established counterparts in York Region (18.1 per cent).

With regard to country of origin (that is, place of birth), 72 per cent of the recent immigrants came from ten countries: seven countries in Asia (China, Iran, India, South Korea, Sri Lanka, Pakistan, and Philippines) and three countries in Eastern Europe (Russia, Ukraine, and Romania), all non-traditional source countries (table 3.3). Immigrants from mainland China, who make up the largest single group of recent immigrants, have settled in a well-established community where recent immigrants are only a third of the population. In contrast, of the immigrants from the Russian Federation, approximately two-thirds are recent immigrants.

The size and history of immigrant groups influence settlement processes. While recent immigrants benefit initially from being part of a large and established community, over the long run those who are more isolated learn Canada's official languages more quickly and have greater economic success (Beiser 1999). The settlement trends in York Region suggest that some immigrant groups may integrate more quickly than others.

Successful settlement often depends on learning one of Canada's official languages. Most of the recent immigrants in York Region, with the exception of those from India and the Philippines, come from societies that do not use English or French as a major language of instruction in schools. Therefore, the majority of adult recent immigrants would likely need language instruction after arrival in Canada. Yet the 2006 census data show that 84 per cent of recent immigrants in the region reported some knowledge of English; only 11 per cent reported speaking neither English nor French (table 3.4). Since official language ability is self-reported, these statistics from the census may not be a good

Table 3.3   Recent immigrants in York Region from top ten places of birth, 2006

Place of birth	All immigrants		Recent immigrants		Recent immigrants as % of all immigrants
	N	%	N	%	
China	86,830	9.8	28,000	25.6	32.2
Mainland	40,255	4.5	18,180	16.6	45.2
Hong Kong	46,575	5.3	9,820	9.0	21.1
Iran	16,905	1.9	9,175	8.4	54.3
India	22,910	2.6	8,500	7.8	37.1
Russian Federation	11,255	1.3	7,555	6.9	67.1
Korea, South	8,860	1.0	5,060	4.6	57.1
Sri Lanka	13,945	1.6	4,935	4.5	35.4
Pakistan	8,015	0.9	4,655	4.3	58.1
Philippines	13,570	1.5	4,150	3.8	30.6
Ukraine	6,725	0.8	4,025	3.7	59.9
Romania	5,230	0.6	2,720	2.5	52.0
Top 10 countries	194,245	22.0	78,775	72.1	40.6
All countries	380,375	100.0	109,270	100.0	28.7

Source: Statistics Canada 2008

measure of English proficiency. Indeed, being able to conduct basic conversations may not be sufficient to meet the language requirements demanded for many jobs.

Poverty is more prominent among York Region's recent immigrant population than in the total population; in 2006 the average household income for recent immigrants was only 70 per cent of that for the total population. Overall, 27 per cent of recent immigrants lived in low-income households, more than double the percentage in the total population. This explains why, of the 109,270 immigrants who had been in Canada for less than ten years, 47 per cent spent over 30 per cent of their household income on housing, and 25 per cent spent 50 per cent or more of their household income on housing (compared with 26 per cent and 12 per cent, respectively, for the total population).

Table 3.4   Recent immigrants in York Region by knowledge of official languages, 2006

Knowledge of official languages	Total population		Recent immigrants	
	N	%	N	%
English only	786,595	88.7	92,240	84.4
French only	570	0.1	150	0.1
Both English and French	64,105	7.2	5,110	4.7
Neither English nor French	35,305	4.0	11,775	10.8

Source: Statistics Canada 2008

Seniors

Seniors are people who are sixty-five years of age and older. In 2006, 87,620 seniors resided in York Region, an increase of 37 per cent over 2001. The senior population accounted for 10 per cent of the region's total population. Three-quarters of the seniors in York Region were either born in Canada (30 per cent) or immigrated before 1980 (45 per cent); only 8 per cent were recent immigrants. The seniors were more likely to be women (54 per cent) and less educated than the total population; over 40 per cent had less than nine years of schooling, compared to 19 per cent in the total population. Almost one-fifth admitted that they had no knowledge of either English or French; they were as likely to be established immigrants born in Italy, Greece, or Poland as they were recent immigrants from China or India.

While most seniors had retired, 14 per cent were still in the labour force. Over half of them worked part time, and more than a third were self-employed; these rates were much higher than those in the total population, although the proportion that was unemployed (3.8 per cent) was slightly lower (5.4 per cent). Their industrial and occupational distributions reflected those of the total population; close to 50 per cent of those active in the labour market were in manufacturing, construction, trade, and support services, and 40 per cent had unskilled or, at best, semi-skilled jobs, suggesting that these were survival jobs.

Generally speaking, the seniors in York Region were economically not so disadvantaged; the percentage living below the low-income cut-off point was slightly below that for the population as a whole. Their median individual and household incomes in 2006, at $20,366 and $66,289, respectively, were about 70 per cent of the regional average. As expected, nearly all received some form of income from the government, such as Canada Pension Plan (CPP) or the low-income supplement. Yet compared to less than a third in the total population, over half of the seniors had income from dividends, interest, and other investment income. They mostly owned their home and, relative to the total population, spent less on housing.

A concern is that three out of ten seniors did not live with their immediate family, and over half of the seniors, in fact, lived alone. It would seem that they are more vulnerable and can make use of more social programs and supports.

Low-Income Persons

In 2006, 112,165 people or 12.7 per cent of York Region's population had low incomes, a 55 per cent increase over 2001, when the low-income population was 10 per cent of the total population in the region. Their median income was $8,846 for an individual and $23,478 for a household, about a third of the regional medians.

Compared to the total population, the proportion of women with low incomes was higher than the proportion of men with low incomes. While the proportion of seniors in the low-income population (9.5 per cent) was comparable to the proportion of seniors in the total population (9.9 per cent), the proportions of those under twenty-four years of age and those between thirty-five and forty-four years of age who were living in low-income households were higher than the proportion of those age groups as a whole in the region. This suggests two things. Adults can benefit from more training and employment-related services. Children in low-income households are especially vulnerable. The growing trend in poverty suggests that services for children and youth are crucial.

Generally, people on lower incomes have lower levels of education. It is, however, alarming to discover that close to half of the low-income individuals in York Region had post-secondary education and that both the number and the proportion (two out of five) with the highest level of education (that is, at least one university degree) more than doubled between 2001 and 2006, and these figures were much higher than in the total population.

It has been widely reported that recent immigrants are more likely to be living in poverty than are the Canadian born (Picot, Hou, and Coulombe 2008). A quarter of the regional low-income population immigrated to Canada between 2001 and 2006. Of the low-income population, people of Chinese ethnic origin accounted for the highest percentage (25 per cent), followed by about 10 per cent each of Italian, English, and Canadian ethnic origin, and about 5 per cent each of Irish, Scottish, East Indian, Iranian, Korean, Jewish, and Russian origins. People of Korean, Pakistani, Iranian, and, to a lesser extent, Chinese, Sri Lankan, Vietnamese, and Russian ethnic origins were more likely to have low incomes. For example, in 2006, 44 per cent of the Koreans, 37 per cent of the Pakistanis, 28 per cent of the Iranians, 19 per cent of the Chinese, 18 per cent of the Sri Lankans, 16 per cent of the Vietnamese, and 15 per cent of the Russians lived below the low-income cut-off point, compared with 12.7 per cent in the general population.

Examination of the place of birth shows that the Canadian-born population accounted for the largest percentage (41 per cent) of low-income individuals, although high percentages of certain immigrant groups lived in poverty. As table 3.5 shows, half of those born in Korea, a third of those born in Pakistan and Taiwan, a quarter of those born in Iran and China, and a fifth of those from Hong Kong, Russia, and Ukraine lived in poverty. An alarming trend is that for the majority of birthplaces, the low-income population is increasing. The only exceptions are immigrants from Hong Kong, Italy, Taiwan, and the United States. For three of these cases – Hong Kong, Italy, and the United States – the majority arrived before 1996. Since income tends to increase with residence in Canada, well-established immigrants are less likely to have low incomes than are recently arrived immigrants. Taiwanese immigrants do not fit this pattern, because many are recent arrivals.[3]

Adults with low incomes are less likely to participate in the paid labour force. In 2006, when 70 per cent of the total population aged fifteen years and over were in the labour force, the labour-force participation rate for those with low incomes was only 55 per cent. In addition to lower labour-force participation, there were proportionally many more part-time workers and self-employed individuals among those with low incomes (table 3.6). Table 3.6 also shows that there were proportionally more low-income people in occupations characterized as

---

3 Ley (2010) has discussed the challenges of assessing the poverty of recent immigrants. He notes that some Hong Kong immigrants are asset rich but income poor. Although they arrived with sufficient assets to purchase housing, cars, and other necessities, they report low annual incomes because of the challenges of finding Canadian jobs commensurate with their qualifications and expertise.

Table 3.5 Top twenty birthplaces of low-income individuals

	Total population 2006	Low-income population 2006	% of total in low-income 2006	Change in low-income population 2001–2006	Change in proportion of low-income 2001–2006
All places of birth	886,575	112,165	100.0	39,595	2.6
Canada	497,715	46,290	9.3	16,075	2.4
China	40,255	10,190	25.3	5,025	2.5
Hong Kong	46,575	9,575	20.6	−845	−3.3
Iran	16,905	4,890	28.9	3,045	6.4
Korea, South	8,860	4,325	48.8	2,340	6.7
Italy	40,105	3,320	8.3	−720	−2.2
Pakistan	8,015	2,800	34.9	1,550	7.8
Sri Lanka	13,945	2,415	17.3	2,035	10.8
India	22,910	2,410	10.5	1,220	2.2
Russian Federation	11,255	2,255	20.0	1,020	1.1
Philippines	13,570	1,925	14.2	1,000	2.7
United Kingdom	18,235	1,560	8.6	5	0.8
Ukraine	6,725	1,330	19.8	820	4.7
Vietnam	9,025	1,170	13.0	655	0.5
Taiwan	3,680	1,115	30.3	215	−4.3
Israel	5,910	1,085	18.4	655	8.6
United States	7,040	990	14.1	−5	−3.4
Jamaica	8,435	970	11.5	325	2.4
Guyana	6,295	625	9.9	160	2.3
Greece	4,760	570	12.0	210	4.7

Source: Statistics Canada 2008

unskilled or semi-skilled, including those in support services and the accommodation and food industry as opposed to the sectors of finance and real estate; government, education, health, and social assistance; and professional and management.

Almost all low-income individuals in 2006 relied on some form of government transfer payment, be it CPP, employment insurance, or welfare. Compared to the total population, a much higher proportion

Table 3.6   Low-income individuals in the labour market, 2006

	Total population in York Region		Low-income population in York Region	
	No.	%	No.	%
Total population	886,575	100.0	112,165	100.0
Labour-force participation	499,720	70.5	47,250	54.8
Part-time workers	175,925	37.2	22,705	53.9
Self-employed	68,275	14.4	11,700	27.8
Unemployed	282,700	5.4	15,640	10.9
All industries	472,610	98.4	42,090	94.9
Primary	6,130	1.3	300	0.7
Manufacturing and construction	94,315	20.0	7,965	18.9
Wholesale and retail trade	86,165	18.2	8,430	20.0
Transportation and warehousing	16,500	3.5	2,055	4.9
Information and cultural industries	14,410	3.0	840	2.0
Finance and real estate	46,340	9.8	3,070	7.3
Professional and management	49,445	10.5	3,290	7.8
Support and other services	41,490	8.8	5,900	14.0
Government, education, health, and social assistance	84,400	17.9	4,740	11.3
Arts and entertainment, accommodation, and food	33,425	7.1	5,510	13.1
All occupations	472,610	98.4	42,090	94.9
Senior management	32,540	6.9	1,590	3.8
Middle and other management	35,675	7.5	3,640	8.6
Skill level 4 (professionals)	100,990	21.4	4,715	11.2
Skill level 3 (semi-professionals, technical ...)	50,060	10.6	3,690	8.8
Skill level 3 (supervisors, skilled crafts ...)	65,325	13.8	6,745	16.0
Skill level 2 (clerical, sales and services)	107,010	22.6	10,490	24.9
Skill level 2 (semi-skilled manual workers)	32,535	6.9	3,810	9.1
Skill level 1 (manual workers ...)	48,490	10.3	7,410	17.6

Source: Statistics Canada 2008

of low-income individuals also received income from self-employment, suggesting the possible survival nature of self-employment among the economically disadvantaged. The income composition of the low-income population changed over recent years; fewer people earned wages and salaries, more received government transfer payments or had investment income, and those with self-employment income and/or income from other sources doubled or more (table 3.7).

Owing to the lack of rental housing, the rate of homeownership in York Region is high. Three-quarters of the low-income population lived in owned dwellings, and more than 60 per cent were spending at least 50 per cent of their household income on mortgage payments; this percentage is very high compared to 12 per cent in the total population and 25 per cent in the recent immigrant population.

Similar to recent immigrants, the majority of those living with low incomes were concentrated in the southern municipalities of Vaughan, Richmond Hill, and Markham. Parts of Georgina and Aurora also had high concentrations of this population. Spatially, people living with low incomes were increasingly spread across the region. For example, Vaughan has seen its low-income population spreading from the southwestern corner to the northeastern corner of the municipality since 2001 (figure 3.4).

Investigating Vulnerability and Social Services

Social services can help alleviate vulnerability and inequality (DeBresson and Barker 1998; Murie and Musterd 2004). The following four chapters assess the accessibility of education, employment, housing, and settlement services to seniors, recent immigrants, and low-income persons in York Region, as well as these vulnerable groups' awareness of, use of, and satisfaction with those services. Several sources of data are used, including customized 2006 Canadian census data, an inventory of social infrastructure in York Region, and a survey administered to residents of York Region.

Access to Social Services

Access to social services is examined by comparing where people live (demand) and where social services are available (supply). The 2006 census shows where the three vulnerable groups lived in York Region. The location of social services was gathered from community-based

Table 3.7   Sources of income for low-income individuals, 2001 and 2006

	2001		2006	
	No.	%	No.	%
Receiving income	48,745	67.2	76,425	68.1
From wages and salaries	20,455	42.0	29,085	38.1
From self-employment	4,335	8.9	12,160	15.9
From government sources	42,155	86.5	71,015	92.9
From dividends, interest, and other investment	10,050	20.6	20,300	26.6
From other income (e.g., retirement pension)	2,375	4.9	8,450	11.1

Source: Statistics Canada 2008

and official sources. The Community Information and Volunteer Centre (CIVC) was an online service that contained a relatively comprehensive list of human service providers in York Region. Listed for each service provider were its full address, the services offered, and the languages spoken by its staff. For this research a list of all education, employment, housing, and settlement service providers that was posted on their website as of December 2006 was extracted. Education service locations were supplemented by online data managed by the York Region Public School Board, the York Region Catholic School Board, and the York Region website. Additional information on settlement services was provided by Citizenship and Immigration Canada (2009) and York Region Human Services Planning Coalition (2007). Together they built the York Infrastructure Database.

In order to assess how easily recent immigrants, seniors, and low-income residents in York Region can reach education, employment, housing, and settlement services in the region, several spatial analytic techniques – such as catchment area analysis, shortest path analysis, neighbourhood opportunity analysis, and accessibility indices (see Fotheringham and Rogerson 2008; Ghosh and Ingene 1991; Longley and Clarke 1995) – are used to map and count each type of service available to each vulnerable group in each municipality and to examine the geographic match between the locations of the vulnerable populations and those of the social services. Since vulnerable individuals often do not have access to a car, and many use public transit to reach service providers (Heisz and Schellenberg 2004; Lo, Shalaby, and Alshalafah 2012), the analyses are based on the assumptions that people walk along the street network at four kilometres an hour to reach a bus stop, and buses run at thirty kilometres an hour, to account for wait and transfer times.

Although the data used for analysing accessibility are tremendously rich, like all other data they have limitations. Appropriate information on the size and capacity of the service providers (except in the case of language instruction for recent immigrants), the quality of service provided, the transit schedules, and the speed limits imposed on the streets and roads in York Region, if available, would have enriched the analyses. Ideally, the accessibility potential of the vulnerable populations, based on income and car ownership or access, should have been calculated to paint a better portrait of their mobility. These problems are not unique to this study, although it means that the accessibility measures are primarily distance based (Apparicio, Cloutier, and Shearmur 2007; Wang and Truelove 2003).

Service Awareness, Use, and Satisfaction

To evaluate the awareness of, use of, and satisfaction with social services in York Region, a questionnaire survey of residents was conducted in two phases: a random phase and a purposeful phase. The random phase focused on census tracts that contained large numbers of immigrants and ethnic groups, persons speaking English as a second language, seniors, and people with low incomes. It was augmented by purposeful sampling when the random strategy did not produce sufficient numbers of persons in each vulnerable population who were using the services under study. The purposeful sample was based on referrals from service providers. In total, 1,546 persons participated in the survey, of which 1,095 were selected randomly and 451 purposefully.

Besides demographics, the survey questionnaire probed respondents about their length of residence in York Region and their satisfaction with living there; their immigrant status, including place of birth, year of immigration, age at immigration, and immigration class; their household composition; their children's education and childcare needs; their employment status and the services they have used; their housing problems and the services they have used; their use of settlement services if they were immigrants; their use of seniors' centres and services if they were seniors; and their awareness of, use of, and satisfaction with services provided by specific service providers. The survey provided rich information on who used and who did not use services, which services were relevant for each group, and whether there was a perceived need for each service.

There are distinct differences in the characteristics of respondents between the random and the purposeful samples. Over 50 per cent in each sample had a university education. The purposeful sample contained a higher proportion of women (68 per cent versus 56 per cent), seniors (27 per cent versus 11 per cent), and recent immigrants (72 per cent versus 27 per cent). Compared to the purposeful sample, the random sample indicated higher household income ($75,000 versus $20,000), but this can be masked by a higher proportion refusing to supply information (38 per cent versus 11 per cent).

Table 3.8 lists the use of various services by respondents in different vulnerable groups. The frequent use of education services, which was compulsory for children until the age of sixteen at the time of the survey, stands out. For every group, except recent immigrants who have low incomes and those who are seniors, education services are the most frequently used type of service. Few respondents use housing services, perhaps because of the limited supply of rental and subsidized housing in the region. As expected, seniors and recent immigrants are more likely to use the services targeted at them. Recent immigrants are also the most likely to use employment services. Established immigrants who have lived in Canada for more than ten years, and Canadian-born residents, are more likely to use employment services than housing services.

Table 3.8   Respondents in vulnerable populations by use of services

	Number in full sample	Using education services (%)	Using employment services* (%)	Using housing services (%)	Using settlement services (%)	Using seniors services (%)
Total	1,546	64.4	16.7	4.9	11.1	4.3
Seniors	235	88.9	0.9	6.0	3.0	28.2
Low-income seniors	42	73.8	2.4	14.3	4.8	45.2
Low-income**	214	51.4	25.2	12.1	27.1	8.9
Recent immigrants (RI)	540	48.0	23.0	5.4	31.9	3.5
Low-income RI	133	36.8	25.6	10.5	43.6	7.5
Senior RI	51	23.5	2.0	5.9	13.7	37.3
Established immigrants***	640	75.8	12.8	4.2	NA	6.4
Canadian-born	336	64.0	13.7	5.7	NA	1.8

*   Including any services related to paid employment, self-employment, unemployment, and other employment-related matters.
**   Drawing on Statistics Canada's low-income cut-offs, *low income* is defined as individuals living in single-person households with annual income below $20,000 and individuals living in multi-person households with annual household income below $30,000.
***   Established immigrants have been living in Canada for more than ten years. The total subsample of 640 includes 17 who did not remember when they immigrated to Canada.
Source: Authors' Survey 2008

4 Education Infrastructure in York Region

Introduction

As a social equalizer, education infrastructure represents institutions for social change, transformation, and justice in democratic societies. As a lifelong learning process, education, broadly defined, includes early-childhood education, primary and secondary schooling, post-secondary education, and continuing education for adults. The provision, maintenance, and governance of education infrastructure in Ontario is accordingly multifaceted and complexly organized. Education is both a public and a private good; although formally it is governed by policy guidelines and statutory regulations at all levels of government, informally it also involves community engagement and the production of local social and cultural capital in its day-to-day activities.

During the past decade, public education across Western democracies has faced a number of challenges with the neoliberalization of education systems. This has resulted in many changes, including severe cutbacks, crowded classrooms, school closures, reduced after-school activities, and privatization and marketization of the education system as a whole in Ontario. These rapid changes in education provision over the past few years have consequently affected those who are most vulnerable, and different regions across the province have adjusted to the changes in different ways. The economic crisis that began in 2009 and the increasing levels of unemployment suggest that education services will be in even greater demand. These past and future conditions need to be borne in mind in considerations of the way in which education infrastructure can shape the landscape of opportunity in York Region. The gaps and their effects on marginal groups of citizens are often most clearly evident through the education system's spatial manifestations, where the demand for and the supply of education services do not often coherently or equitably correspond.

Education infrastructure in York Region faces a number of unique challenges based on the complexities of its heterogeneous landscape. Intersecting urban, suburban, and rural developments, augmented by rapidly changing demographic shifts, increasing cultural diversity, and social polarization, collectively defy traditional suburban imaginaries of uniformity and homogeneity. These stereotypes often lead to the misallocation and distribution of scarce resources, affecting a marginal population that is often inconspicuous as a result. This chapter explores the state of education infrastructure in York Region, noting in particular the spatial distribution of education services, while highlighting education provision as it relates to the three vulnerable groups in this study – recent immigrants, seniors, and low-income persons.

In four sections this chapter provides information about vulnerable groups of children in York Region and a broad overview of the education services available in York Region and examines the representational provision of education services for recent immigrants, seniors, and low-income persons, and their awareness and use of education services in York Region.

Marginal Groups in Perspective

In 2006, 12.7 per cent (112,165) of the population in York Region was designated low income, and these individuals reported a median household income of $23,478. Many are seniors and recent immigrants who would benefit from continuing education and training opportunities. The highest percentage of low-income population (23.3 per cent) within this group was for families with children under fourteen years of age (25,970). The increase in the proportion of those experiencing poverty in York Region (nearly 4 per cent since 2001) is the highest for children, among all age cohorts. In the same year 15.7 per cent of the low-income population was youth of fifteen to twenty-four years of age (17,665). Couples with children represented the majority of low-income families (87.2 per cent), along with single-parent families (17.2 per cent). Combined, children and youth in York Region represent a large vulnerable group (39 per cent) for which publicly funded education opportunities and affordable, high-quality early learning and child-care programs are urgently needed. The dispersal of children in York Region (figure 4.1) creates additional challenges for those responsible for providing education services.

Figure 4.1   Distribution of children and youth in York Region, 2006

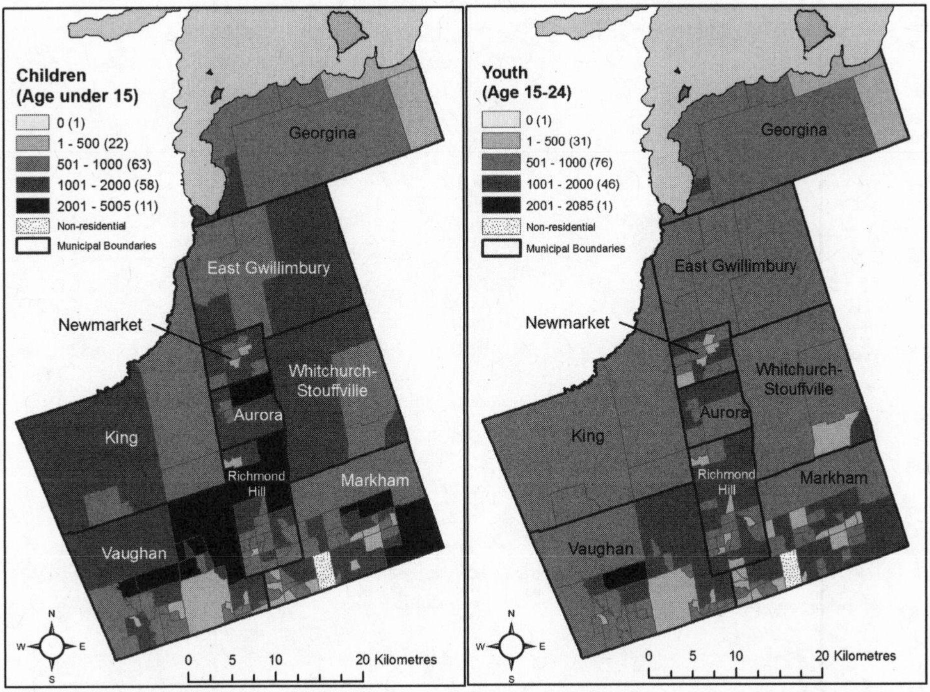

Source: Statistics Canada 2008

Spatial Distribution of Education Infrastructure in York Region

With table 4.1 outlining the different types of education infrastructure in York Region's nine municipalities, and figure 4.2 illustrating the spatial distribution of these services, this chapter describes below, in broad strokes, the spatial patterns of availability.

Early-Childhood Education

Early-childhood education includes a variety of early-learning and childcare settings for children from infancy to school age. Although the value of early-childhood education is well established in the literature,

Table 4.1 Education infrastructure in York Region, 2006

	York Region (N)	Markham (%)	Vaughan (%)	Richmond Hill (%)	Aurora (%)	New-market (%)	King (%)	East Gwillimbury (%)	Whitchurch-Stouffville (%)	Georgina (%)
YRDSB* elementary	142	33.1	14.8	15.5	7.0	11.3	4.2	3.5	2.1	8.5
YCDSB** elementary	71	25.4	39.4	9.9	7.0	8.5	4.2	2.8	2.8	4.2
YRDSB secondary	28	28.6	17.9	17.9	7.1	14.3	3.6		3.6	7.1
YCDSB secondary	12	33.3	33.3	8.3	8.3	8.3				8.3
YRDSB Hub	4	50.0			25.0	25.0				
YCDSB Hub	1				100.0					
French public	3	33.3			66.7					
Preschool	38	10.5	34.2	21.1	5.3	2.6	7.9	10.5		7.9
Private Montessori	6		50.0			16.7	16.7	16.7		
Post-secondary	4	25.0		25.0		25.0	25.0			
Other tutoring	35	14.3	11.4	22.9	5.7	31.4	5.7	2.9		5.7

* York Region District School Board
** York Catholic District School Board

Source: CIVC 2006

Figure 4.2 Education infrastructure in York Region, 2006

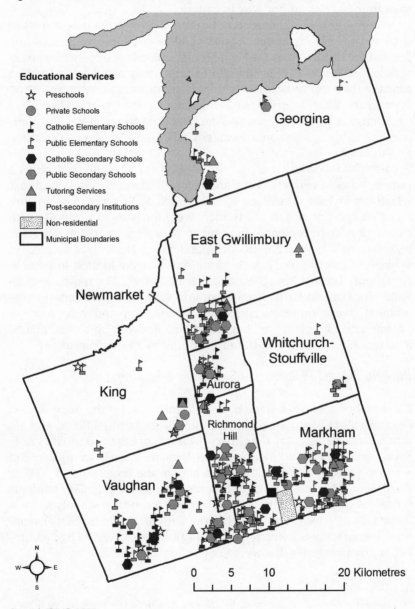

Source: CIVC 2006

the care and education of children less than six years of age continues to be funded in an ad hoc way in Ontario.

Investing in early-childhood education is considered one of the key determinants of human development and health; for low-income families and the children of recent immigrants, an early start provides an equitable foundation in education. In Ontario, early-childhood education can take the form of licensed regulated childcare, in-home care, or informal care. Licensed childcare is regulated by the Ontario Ministry of Children and Youth Services, and the standards are set in the *Day Nurseries Act* (http://www.ontario.ca/education-and-training/education-and-training).

Early-childhood education in York Region includes childcare centres, nursery schools, extended care, and before- and after-school programs, which can include subsidized spaces funded by the provincial government. At the time of this study there were thirty-eight licensed childcare centres in the region; 34 per cent of these were located in Vaughan, followed by 21 per cent in Richmond Hill.[1] None was located in Whitchurch-Stouffville. The childcare centres were located in schools, community centres, churches, and private homes. The region also offered four Ontario Early Years programs. Created by the Ontario government, these programs provided information and resources for parents and caregivers on parenting and networking (http://www.ontario.ca/education-and-training/education-and-training).

Publicly Funded Primary and Secondary Schooling

Public schools in York Region are administered by the York Region District School Board and York Catholic District School Board and are funded and regulated by the Ontario Ministry of Education. With growing diversity and rapid increases in enrolment, there is an urgent need for new schools, resources, and teachers in the region. As of 2007–8, there were 111,556 elementary students and 56,773 secondary students served by 275 elementary schools and 60 secondary schools in York Region. The Conseil Scolaire de District Catholique Centre-Sud also operated three schools in the region. In addition, York Region had a number of private schools that were not publicly funded.

---

1 There is no means of enumerating the unlicensed childcare centres operating in the region that have been the subject of recent newspaper reports (Ballingall 2013).

YORK REGION DISTRICT SCHOOL BOARD

In 2007–8 York Region District School Board (YRDSB) served over 113,000 students in 192 schools. As the third-largest school board in Ontario, it has opened 83 new elementary schools and 15 new secondary schools since 1998–9. New schools have been built in each municipality, although there has been a noticeable concentration in Markham, which has had a 35 per cent increase in the number of elementary schools and a 32 per cent increase in the number of secondary schools. The most recent expansion has eased the pressure on enrolment levels. The YRDSB actively promotes a policy on anti-racism and ethno-cultural equity (http://www.yrdsb.edu.on.ca) that emphasizes the importance of

- respecting the racial and ethno-cultural diversity of its students, community, and employees;
- recognizing the potential for academic excellence in all students;
- providing necessary supports so that the academic achievement of every student, regardless of race, ethnicity, culture, faith, language, and nationality, is consistent with the student's highest ability;
- ensuring equitable treatment for all students, parents, and employees while recognizing their race, ethnicity, culture, faith, language, and nationality;
- working to achieve equitable results in its educational and employment practices; and
- promoting positive and respectful relations with and between members of all school communities.

These broad guidelines apply to board policies and practices; leadership; school-community partnerships; curriculum; student languages; student evaluation, assessment, and placement; guidance; racial and ethno-cultural harassment; employment and promotion practices; and staff development.

In addition to its elementary and secondary schools, the YRDSB offers services in four hubs. They include Alternative Education programs, English as a Second Language (ESL) for adults, Community and Cultural Services, International Co-op, School-to-Work Transition programs, Special Education, and Youth Apprenticeship.

YORK CATHOLIC DISTRICT SCHOOL BOARD

Catholic schools primarily serve the children of Roman Catholic parents, or students who have been baptized Roman Catholic. In 2007–8 the York Catholic District School Board (YCDSB) served over 55,000 students in 106 schools. It had opened 21 elementary schools and 14 secondary schools since 1998–9, resulting in a 17 per cent increase in elementary schools and a 92 per cent increase in secondary schools. Most of the growth was concentrated in Vaughan and Markham. The enrolment levels by school (crowding index) have fallen dramatically in secondary schools since 2001–2 (see table 4.2). Nevertheless, 299 portable classrooms remained in 2008. Like the YRDSB, the YCDSB has a policy on anti-racism and ethno-cultural equity incorporated in its mission statement and core objectives. The broad guidelines are similar to those promoted by the YRDSB.

The YCDSB offered additional services in one hub; these include Adult and Continuing Education (New-Canadian Program), Alternative Education programs, ESL for adults, International Student Exchange, Special Education, and Youth Apprenticeship.

Post-Secondary Schooling

Seneca College of Applied Arts and Technology operates three campuses in York Region that offer programs in science, technology, and business, as well as opportunities for academic upgrading and college preparation. Of note are the two campuses in Newmarket and Richmond Hill that offer the Job Connect program, a career and employment preparation program funded by the Ontario Ministry of Training, Colleges, and Universities for youth and adults.

Adult Continuing Education

Adult education programs, including general-interest courses and credit courses, are offered through both the public and the Catholic school boards in the evening and in the Richmond Hill Community Centre as day programs; some courses are offered online. At the time of this study there were twenty-five Adult ESL day classes offered across the region in schools, churches, and libraries. Adult ESL evening classes were offered in seventeen high schools in the region. The school boards also offer specialized programs, such as Citizenship Classes, Driver Education, Adult Literacy and Basic Skills, Language Instruction for Newcomers to Canada, Ontario High School Equivalency Certificate (GED), and International Programs (http://www.yrdsb.edu.on.ca).

Table 4.2 Enrolment by school in York Region, 1998–2008

	York Region District School Board		York Catholic District School Board	
	Number of schools	Average enrolment per school	Number of schools	Average enrolment per school
Elementary				
1998–9	109	499	62	500
1999–2000	111	508	65	491
2000–1	116	509	68	484
2001–2	118	522	70	493
2007–8	192	386	83	450
Secondary				
1998–9	22	2,473	9	3,446
1999–2000	23	2,453	9	3,546
2000–1	24	2,460	10	3,292
2001–2	25	2,463	11	3,136
2007–8	37	1,056	23	770

Source: Ministry of Education (special request)

Geographies of Vulnerable Groups and Education Infrastructure

To evaluate access to educational opportunities the spatial distribution of education infrastructure was compared with the residential pattern of each vulnerable group by calculating a representation index. The percentage of facilities in census tracts with high numbers of a vulnerable group was compared to that of facilities in all census tracts. For example, there are thirty high-immigrant census tracts. In those thirty tracts there are thirty-three YRDSB elementary schools, which make up 23.2 per cent of all elementary schools under the board's jurisdiction. Representation was calculated as the ratio of the percentage of schools in high-immigrant census tracts to the percentage of schools in all census tracts. A value of 1.0 indicates that the two distributions – one for census tracts with a large vulnerable population and the other for all census tracts – are the same. Values below 1.0 indicate under-representation of facilities, and values above 1.0 reveal over-representation.

Recent Immigrants and Education Infrastructure

According to the 2006 census, four census tracts, primarily in Markham, contained a high concentration of recent immigrants (over one thousand), and twenty-six tracts were home to between five hundred and one thousand recent immigrants. These thirty census tracts lie primarily within Markham, Vaughan, and Richmond Hill. Table 4.3 shows that elementary schools were well- to over-represented in these high-immigrant tracts, with representation indices ranging from 1.04 to 2.98. Catholic secondary schools were under-represented, as were the number of preschool (kindergarten) programs compared to those in the rest of the region. More investment in preschool programs in these census tracts would be beneficial for young children.

Seniors and Education Infrastructure

In 2006 high numbers of seniors (over one thousand) lived in ten census tracts scattered across the region, in southeast Markham (three), Vaughan (three), Georgina (one), Whitchurch-Stouffville (one), Newmarket (one), and Richmond Hill (one). Eighty-five other census tracts had between five hundred and one thousand seniors. Proximity to secondary schools, which sometimes host free and low-cost continuing education programs, would be very useful for seniors. Intergenerational programs in preschools and elementary schools and parenting (or grandparenting) centres also provide the opportunity to foster more community engagement. However, spatial analysis revealed that elementary schools and preschools were slightly over-represented in the tracts with large numbers of seniors, while public secondary schools were not (table 4.4). As for post-secondary institutions, the Seneca College location in Newmarket provides educational opportunities to the high concentration of seniors living nearby.

Low-Income Persons and Education Infrastructure

Thirty-six census tracts in 2006 were home to more than one thousand low-income persons, mainly in Markham, Vaughan, Richmond Hill, and Georgina. In these tracts both public elementary and secondary schools were well represented. Catholic high schools, however, were under-represented, even though Catholic elementary schools were over-represented in these census tracts. There were a large number of French public schools in census tracts close to the City of Toronto.

Table 4.3   Education infrastructure and recent immigrants, 2006

	Number of schools in high-immigrant census tracts	Number in all census tracts	Per cent of schools in high-immigrant census tracts	Representation
YRDSB elementary	33	142	23.24	1.04
YCDSB elementary	20	71	28.17	1.26
YRDSB secondary	6	28	21.43	0.96
YCDSB secondary	1	12	8.33	0.37
French public schools	2	3	66.67	2.98
Preschools	4	38	10.53	0.47·
Post-secondary	0	4	0.00	0.89
No. of census tracts with educational institutions	30	134	22.39	

Source: CIVC 2006; Statistics Canada 2008

Table 4.4   Education infrastructure and seniors, 2006

	Number in high-senior census tracts	Number in all census tracts	Per cent in high-senior census tracts	Representation
YRDSB elementary	14	142	9.86	1.32
YCDSB elementary	12	71	16.90	2.26
YRDSB secondary	2	28	7.14	0.96
YCDSB secondary	0	12	0.00	0.00
French public schools	0	3	0.00	0.00
YRDSB hub	0	4	0.00	0.00
YCDSB hub	0	1	0.00	0.00
Preschools	4	38	10.53	1.41
Post-secondary	1	4	25.00	1.15
No. of census tracts with educational institutions	10	134	7.46	

Source: CIVC 2006; Statistics Canada 2008

As table 4.5 shows, there were few preschools in neighbourhoods with large low-income populations. As expected, private schools, including Montessori schools, were under-represented in these neighbourhoods, as the costs of attending them are usually prohibitive for low-income families. Interestingly, the presence of tutoring schools is nearly at par with the rest of the region.

Use of Education Services

The telephone survey aimed to gauge the factors that influence awareness of, access to, and satisfaction with education services among the vulnerable groups. Of the 1,546 respondents, only 11.2 per cent had lived in York Region all their lives. Nearly 50 per cent had lived in the region for six years or less, while 20 per cent had lived there for over sixteen years. More than a third of respondents were recent immigrants who had arrived in Canada within the past ten years. These newcomers had moved to York Region for affordable housing (14.1 per cent), good quality housing (11.1 per cent), neighbourhood amenities (18.5 per cent), and work (12.4 per cent). A few had relocated to be closer to people from the same ethnic or cultural background (6.4 per cent), their parents (7.2 per cent), or better educational opportunities (8.6 per cent).

In the previous five years a large number of respondents (35.3 per cent) had taken some training or language courses, although their interest in continuing education was not satisfied. Over 28 per cent of respondents were interested in taking additional training or language courses. Most respondents said that they had received information on courses from friends, family members, or employers and co-workers (48.5 per cent), and 27 per cent obtained information from agencies, organizations, the Internet, YorkLink, CIVC, and media outlets. Most courses were taken at community colleges or universities (23.4 per cent), community agencies or immigrant-serving organizations (18.3 per cent), public elementary or high schools (9.1 per cent), and local community centres (7.5 per cent). About half of the respondents who had taken courses (52 per cent) had paid for them.

Access to a car facilitated the adults' educational activities. Most respondents drove or were driven to their classes (52.3 per cent), some took public transit (28.2 per cent), and a few walked (8.1 per cent). Their reliance on the automobile, combined with the large number of public and Catholic educational facilities in the region, led to short travel times. It took nearly half of the respondents (48.6 per cent) twenty-five

Table 4.5   Education infrastructure and low income, 2006

	Number in high low-income census tracts	Number in all census tracts	Per cent in high low-income census tracts	Representation
YRDSB elementary	36	142	25.35	1.30
YCDSB elementary	25	71	35.21	1.81
YRDSB secondary	9	28	32.14	1.65
YCDSB secondary	1	12	8.33	0.43
French public schools	2	3	66.67	3.42
YRDSB hub	1	4	25.00	1.28
YCDSB hub	0	1	0.00	0.00
Preschools	4	38	10.53	0.54
Tutoring	9	35	25.71	1.32
Post-secondary	1	4	25.00	1.30
No. of census tracts with educational institutions	36	154	26.87	

Source: CIVC 2006; Statistics Canada 2008

minutes or less to reach their destination. Time rather than distance was the major deterrent to adult participation in courses and training. Approximately 58 per cent of respondents had not taken any courses during the past five years because of time constraints, while only 13 per cent cited affordability as their main concern, and even fewer (4.3 per cent) cited distance. Nearly 74 per cent of the respondents had children, and of these children, 91 per cent lived at home. Of these, over 56 per cent were less than eighteen years of age: 13.6 per cent were less than five years of age; 20.8 per cent were from six to thirteen years of age; and 22.1 per cent were between thirteen and eighteen years of age. Most respondents reported having children who were attending school in Canada (74.8 per cent). Over 75 per cent of their children attended an early-childhood-education program (10.9 per cent), elementary school (40.0 per cent), or high school (24.5 per cent). Another 20 per cent of respondents' children attended college and university at the time of the survey. The children of many respondents (54.4 per cent) participated in after-school extracurricular activities. Few respondents (only 6.7 per cent) reported that their children used special education services.

Interestingly, ESL and Heritage language programs were equally popular (attended by 14.5 and 14.7 per cent of the students, respectively).

Most children and youth went to local schools. Most of those who go to schools outside the region (about 20 per cent) are likely travelling to post-secondary institutions. Children and youth rely on the automobile to travel to school, but they are less reliant than are adults. Slightly more than one-third of children were dropped off at school by car (35.2 per cent), while a quarter walked (26.6 per cent), and smaller fractions took school buses (17.8 per cent) or public transit (11.1 per cent). The dispersed spatial patterns of education infrastructures and reliance on cars as a major form of transportation reduced travel times. About 50 per cent of the children spent ten minutes or less travelling to school, while 27.5 per cent commuted between ten and thirty minutes, and 9.2 per cent travelled for up to an hour.

Consistent with other studies showing a shortage of social services in York Region (PricewaterhouseCoopers LLP 2006), only 27.4 per cent of the 497 people who responded to questions concerning childcare indicated that they used paid childcare on a regular basis for their children under thirteen years of age. The majority of those who used childcare (over 52 per cent) had children less than five years of age. Over 27 per cent of households depended on family members (spouse, grandparents, in-laws, other family members) for childcare, and another 14 per cent relied on babysitters, nannies, or live-in caregivers. The shortage of funding for social services was evident in the small number of respondents who used subsidized childcare services (only 9.6 per cent).

Parents of preschoolers were even more dependent on transportation by car than were parents of school-aged children. Almost two-thirds of respondents (65.8 per cent) drove their children to childcare, while 15.8 per cent walked. Very few families with young children (only 1.8 per cent) took public transit to childcare. Once again, reliance on the automobile was reflected in short travel times. Travel time to childcare for most respondents (90.3 per cent) was less than twenty minutes.

Not many senior respondents were involved in classes, recreational activities, or day trips (20.4 per cent). Only 6.2 per cent participated in English-language training, 10.4 per cent in arts and crafts classes, 6.2 per cent in dance and music, 4.2 per cent in computer classes, and 2.1 per cent in continuing education. The most popular activity was exercise classes (27.1 per cent). Leisure activities, such as visiting museums, casinos, and historical sites, were also popular among many seniors (35.4 per cent), as were bingo and card playing (18.8 per cent).

Fewer seniors reported visiting libraries (6.2 per cent) or participating in book clubs (2.1 per cent). Many seniors (26 per cent), however, participated in other types of clubs and associations, with over 50 per cent visiting these venues at least once a week.

Summary and Conclusions

Education infrastructure in York Region faces a number of unique challenges based on the heterogeneous landscape of the region: diverse urban, suburban, and rural development; a rapidly changing demographic composition; and increasing cultural diversity and social polarization. Population growth in York Region has created pressing needs for additional investment in education infrastructure. Despite new construction there is an increased reliance on portable classrooms with the growth of enrolments in the publicly funded school systems. In the recent economic crisis when unemployment rose dramatically, interest in education services also increased. Although many people are interested in continuing education to upgrade their qualifications and training, they have insufficient time to do so, and, for a few, limited public transit services also constrain access.

Children and youth in York Region represent a large vulnerable group for whom services and resources need to be provided carefully. Investing in early-childhood education is a key determinant of human development and health, and for low-income families and children of recent immigrants an early start provides much-needed support for an equitable education. Currently the provision of early-childhood education is uneven, with childcare centres being concentrated in Vaughan and Richmond Hill, while none is located in Whitchurch-Stouffville.[2] To ensure equity and to reduce growing vulnerability, there is a need to develop more early-childhood programs especially in neighbourhoods with large numbers of recent immigrants that are currently under-served.

The findings also highlight the importance of promoting awareness of education services to enhance the inclusion of all vulnerable groups. School boards should review current efforts to publicize continuing

---

2 Our study was completed just as the provincial government began to provide funding for full-day junior and senior kindergarten in a minority of publicly funded schools. As full-day education services are made available in every elementary school, early-childhood education will become more available in all parts of the region and for all social groups.

education programs in order to reach recent immigrants, seniors, and low-income households better. Alternative sites for delivering courses and alternative modes of delivery should also be explored to ensure that educational offerings are accessible to all residents of the region.

This chapter emphasizes the importance of publicly funded educational opportunities for children and youth in order to alleviate child poverty; the need for affordable, high-quality early learning and childcare programs, enabling families to work outside the home or receive training; the need for continuing education for adults, including seniors; and the importance of increasing programs for skills upgrading and language training. Transforming publicly funded schools into local and regional community hubs offers numerous possibilities to redress the exclusion experienced by many members of vulnerable groups, who are often socially and physically isolated. For example, networking and training opportunities for low-income people, intergenerational activities for seniors, and social and cultural activities for recent immigrants, located in elementary and secondary schools, all create venues of support. The provision of such educational facilities exemplifies the important role that social infrastructure can play in combating emerging suburban inequalities.

5 Employment Services in York Region

Introduction

Employment growth has followed population growth since the inception of York Region in 1971. Between 1998 and 2006 employment grew at an annual rate of 4.9 per cent, while population grew at an average annual rate of 5.2 per cent. Jobs in York Region employ predominantly full-time workers. Custom data from Statistics Canada show that 62 per cent of the employed in 2006 worked full time. A York Region employment survey documented that 75.7 per cent of employment in the region was full time in 2006 (Regional Municipality of York 2006, 14). At the same time, part-time employment grew from 17.5 per cent in 1998 to 20.4 per cent in 2006, or an increase of 2 per cent between 2001 and 2006 (Statistics Canada 2008). This represents a key trend and is likely related to population growth, which increases the demand for services; service-oriented jobs accounted for approximately 74 per cent of total employment, with the most important sectors being retail and wholesale trade, and personal and business services (Regional Municipality of York 2006, 14–15). The surge in new jobs within York Region has attracted a better-educated workforce as well. Of adult residents, 25 per cent have a university degree, a figure that rises to 33 per cent among those aged 25–64, which is well above the metropolitan, provincial, and national averages. Unemployment in the region is typically a percentage point lower than the average for the Greater Toronto Area, and two points lower than the rate for the City of Toronto (Pembina Institute 2007, 47).

While York Region has a number of large international firms, small businesses are the predominant form of enterprise, with over 93 per cent of firms (as of June 2005) each employing fewer than twenty people. Furthermore, businesses without employees on the payroll accounted for over 62 per cent of the total, reflecting the entrepreneurial nature of the region's growing population (York Region Planning and Development Services Department 2007, 9). However, there is also substantial growth in the number of larger firms employing more than one hundred employees. Between 1999 and 2003 companies with 100 to 199 employees increased by 53 per cent, those with between 200 and 499 employees increased by 92 per cent, and those with over 500 employees increased by 42 per cent. This rate of growth points to a dynamic and healthy economy and suggests that York Region can attract and accommodate new, growing enterprises and support its own enterprises as they expand.

A good job with career-progress prospects comparable to one's qualification and skills is a major concern for most people. Employment and small-business services can improve employment prospects for individuals, and business opportunities for firms. Services for those in the paid-employment sector include individual counselling or organized programs on job search strategies, résumé writing, and interviewing techniques. For the self-employed such services can provide information or programs on how to start a business and how to calculate self-employment benefits.

This chapter focuses on two vulnerable populations in York Region, namely recent immigrants and those with low incomes. Seniors are excluded as most are retired. Children under fifteen years of age are also excluded because they cannot work legally in the paid-labour market. It examines first the labour-market situations of recent immigrants and low-income persons to assess their demand for services, and then their access to employment services, before turning to their awareness of, use of, and satisfaction with such services.

Labour-Market Characteristics of Recent Immigrants and Low-Income Individuals

The labour-market participation of York Region residents is described in terms of four attributes. To begin, class of worker distinguishes among the employed and unemployed, employees and self-employed. Work activity, for those who are employed or actively looking for work, describes whether the person works full time or part time. The industrial sector classifies the main economic activity of the enterprise in which a person works. Occupation, the fourth attribute of employment considered here, differentiates people in the paid-labour market according to their individual activities at work and the educational and professional qualifications required for that employment. Commuting is another important aspect of employment. The prospect of long and costly work trips may discourage some workers – particularly those who have low incomes or those who are seniors looking for part-time employment – from applying for jobs at a distance. The time and the effort associated with the journey to work depend in part on the mode of transportation, which differentiates people who rely on automobiles from those who use public transit and those who use other modes, principally walking and biking. One of the most significant employment effects is income, for the individual worker and for his or her household. The following compares the labour-market attributes of recent immigrants and low-income residents of York Region with each other and with the regional averages.

Class of Worker and Activity

Of the York Region population in 2006, 80 per cent were fifteen years of age or older; this included 86 per cent of its recent immigrants and 77 per cent of its low-income population. Recent immigrants and people with low incomes are less likely than are other residents of working age to participate in the labour market. As shown in table 5.1, the labour-force-participation rates of these two groups, at 68 per cent and 55 per cent respectively, were much lower than the 70 per cent for the entire working-age population in the region. The unemployment rate for the working-age population in York Region (5.4 per cent) was half the unemployment rate for the low-income population (10.9 per cent) and two-thirds of that for the recent immigrant population (7.5 per cent). It is difficult to determine the nature of the relationship, however. At 24.8 per cent, self-employment was much higher among the low-income population than among either the total working-age population or recent immigrants in the region (both around 14 per cent).

Industry and Occupation

Labour-force activities are generally coded by industry and occupation. In 2006, industry was classified using the 1997 North American Industrial Classification System (NAICS), and occupation was coded

Table 5.1 Labour-market characteristics of population subgroups in York Region, 2006

	Total in York Region		Recent immigrants in York Region		Low-income in York Region	
	#	%	#	%	#	%
Total population aged 15 years and over	708,895		94,125		86,195	
Labour-force participation (population 15 years and over)	499,720	70.5	63,965	68.0	47,250	54.8
Paid workers	402,500	80.5	59,190	77.8	29,845	63.2
Self-employed workers	68,275	13.7	9,085	14.2	11,700	24.8
Unpaid family workers	1,830	0.4	375	0.6	545	1.3
Unemployed	282,700	5.4	4,775	7.5	15,640	10.9
Part-time workers	175,925	35.2	25,845	40.0	22,705	48.5
All industries (1997 NAICS)	472,610		59,190		42,090	
Primary	6,130	1.3	485	0.8	300	0.7
Manufacturing and construction	94,315	20.0	12,835	21.7	7,965	18.9
Wholesale and retail trade	86,165	18.2	11,215	18.9	8,430	20.0
Transportation and warehousing	16,500	3.5	2,155	3.6	2,055	4.9
Information and cultural industries	14,410	3.0	1,950	3.3	840	2.0
Finance and real estate	46,340	9.8	4,965	8.4	3,070	7.3
Professional and management	49,445	10.5	7,490	12.7	3,290	7.8
Support and other services	41,490	8.8	5,500	9.3	5,900	14.0
Government, education, health and social assistance	84,400	17.9	7,325	12.4	4,740	11.3
Arts and entertainment, accommodation and food	33,425	7.1	5,280	8.9	5,510	13.1
All occupations (1991 SOC)	472,610		59,190		42,090	
Senior management	32,540	6.9	2,765	4.7	1,590	3.8
Middle and other management	35,675	7.5	3,500	5.9	3,640	8.6
Skill level 4 (professionals)	100,990	21.4	14,975	25.3	4,715	11.2
Skill level 3 (semi-professional, technical)	50,060	10.6	4,305	7.3	3,690	8.8

Table 5.1 Labour-market characteristics of population subgroups in York Region, 2006 (*Cont.*)

	Total in York Region		Recent immigrants in York Region		Low-income in York Region	
	#	%	#	%	#	%
Skill level 3 (supervisors, skilled crafts)	65,325	13.8	6,950	11.7	6,745	16.0
Skill level 2 (clerical, sales and services)	107,010	22.6	13,580	22.9	10,490	24.9
Skill level 2 (semi-skilled manual workers)	32,535	6.9	5,675	9.6	3,810	9.1
Skill level 1 (manual workers)	48,490	10.3	7,440	12.6	7,410	17.6
Mode of transportation to work:						
Car, truck, or van (as driver or passenger)	328,725	85.3	35,900	76.8	21,750	77.5
Public transit	42,715	11.1	8,415	18.0	4,045	14.4
Other method	13,925	3.6	2,410	5.2	2,280	8.1
Income of population 15 years and over:						
Median total income of individuals	$28,830		$16,417		$8,846	
Average total income of individuals	$42,461		$26,656		$9,497	
Median household income	$92,560		$67,456		$23,478	
Average household income	$114,408		$80,596		$26,453	
Source of income of population 15 years and over:						
Without income	215,110	24.3	24,515	22.4	35,745	31.9
Income from wages and salaries	475,375	53.6	57,485	67.8	29,085	38.1
Self-employment income	89,035	10.0	12,530	14.8	12,160	15.9
Income from government sources	386,485	43.6	56,560	66.7	71,015	92.9
Income from dividends, interest, and investments	270,540	30.5	25,990	30.7	20,300	26.6
Other income (retirement pension, etc.)	106,935	12.1	10,185	12.0	8,450	11.1

Source: Statistics Canada 2008

using the 1991 Social Occupation Classification (SOC). Recent immigrants and the low-income population work in different industrial sectors from those of most of the working-age population in York Region.

In 2006 a larger proportion of workers in the entire York Region population (27.7 per cent) than those in the recent immigrant population (20.8 per cent) and in the low-income population (18.6 per cent) were employed in government, education, health and social services, and the finance and real estate industries. Disproportionately more persons in the low-income population (27.1 per cent) than those in the recent immigrant population (18.2 per cent) and York Region working-age population (15.9 per cent) were engaged in support and other services, arts and entertainment, and accommodation and food industries. While proportionately more of the low-income population worked in wholesale and retail trade or transportation and warehousing, proportionately more recent immigrants were engaged in the professional and management industries.The 1991 SOC codes provide insight into the skill level of jobs held by individuals. A comparison of higher-skilled occupations such as senior management and professionals revealed that a larger percentage of the recent immigrant population (25.3 per cent) than the entire working-age York Region population (21.4 per cent) and the low-income population (11.2 per cent) held professional jobs. At the other end of the skills spectrum (for example, clerical, sales, and service; semi-skilled manual and manual workers), larger percentages of low-income persons (51.6 per cent) and recent immigrants (45.1 per cent) were engaged in such occupations compared with the percentage of all working-age individuals in York Region (39.8 per cent).

Mode of Transportation to Work

York Region is a typical outer suburb in that the vast majority of people travel to work by car as drivers or passengers. In 2006 approximately 85 per cent of all workers travelled to their jobs by car, van, or truck. Another 11 per cent used public transit, and less than 4 per cent walked, biked, or used other means. Compared with the trends for the entire working-age population, recent immigrants and the low-income population were less automobile oriented and were more likely to use public transit or other means. Approximately 77 per cent of recent immigrants and low-income residents commuted by automobile, while 18 per cent of recent immigrants and 14 per cent of low-income workers travelled by public transit. Low income may constrain mode choice. Other means of transportation to work that often cost less than public transit were used more by low-income workers (8 per cent) than by other workers.

Income

All income measures (for example, average total income, median household income, average household income) confirmed that recent immigrants had lower incomes than those incomes typical of the region. The low-income population had average and median incomes that were approximately one-quarter of the average and median incomes for the region. By way of illustration, the median household income in 2006 for people fifteen years of age and older in York Region was $92,560; for recent immigrants of the same age, the median household income was $67,456. Considering the average total income for the population fifteen years and older, the findings were similar: the average total income for the York Region population was $42,461, and for recent immigrants was $26,656. Given their patterns of labour-market participation and low incomes, it is not surprising that a much higher percentage of recent immigrants (67 per cent) and people with low incomes (93 per cent) received income from government sources compared with the percentage for York Region residents as a whole (44 per cent).

The labour-market characteristics of workers in York Region underline the growing inequality in the region. In particular, confronted by language, attitudinal, and professional barriers to participating fully in York Region's employment opportunities, recent immigrants have lower rates of employment, higher rates of unemployment, more involvement in part-time work, and over-representation in declining industrial sectors and in low-skilled occupations. In light of these labour-market patterns, it is not surprising that some recent immigrants in the region report low incomes. In 2006, 27.0 per cent of recent immigrants fell within Statistics Canada's low-income cut-off, compared with only 12.7 per cent of the total population.

Employment Service Provision

The supply of employment services is assessed with three standard indicators: availability (that is, the number of service agencies in an area), capacity (for example, facility size, number of staff members, ratio of users to number of agencies or to number of staff members, and level of funding), and accessibility or the ease with which users can get to a service. The York Infrastructure Database compiled for this study contains the location and service information for each service provider. Employment services for low-income persons and recent immigrants need to be examined separately because these two groups have different cultural needs, and their credentials are most often not from the same country. The same can be said of youth and adults; youth, those between fifteen and twenty-four years of age, are more likely than are adults to seek part-time employment. Figure 5.1 shows the employment service providers catering to low-income persons in the region in 2006.

Employment service providers target different clients. The focus of this study is on those providers serving recent immigrants or low-income persons. In total, more service providers targeted low-income individuals than they did recent immigrants, twenty-six versus sixteen. Of these service providers, five also targeted low-income youths, and three targeted recent immigrant youths. In terms of services for immigrants, only Richmond Hill, Markham, and Vaughan had more than two service providers; outside the urban core, despite the presence of fourteen hundred recent immigrant youths and adults, there was not even one service provider specifically offering employment services for this group. For people with low incomes, Aurora was the only municipality with fewer than two employment service providers. Newmarket had eight. Youths living in Aurora and Markham, from either recent-immigrant or low-income households, were not able to find employment help locally, and it is not clear whether they could seek help in another municipality.

Relative availability is measured by ratios representing the number of people living in each area divided by the number of providers offering services in the area. A smaller ratio reflects greater availability of services. The ratios presented in table 5.2 do not, however, take into account the size of service providers, which is a better indicator of service capacity.

When the ratios for each municipality were compared with the ratios for all of York Region, an uneven distribution of services across the region for both recent immigrants and low-income persons emerged. The availability of employment services for adult recent immigrants was greater in Aurora, Newmarket, and Richmond Hill, and for low-income adults in Newmarket, Aurora, and Georgina. Residents in Vaughan and Markham appeared to be underserved. Employment services for

Figure 5.1 Distribution of employment service providers for low-income persons in York Region, 2006

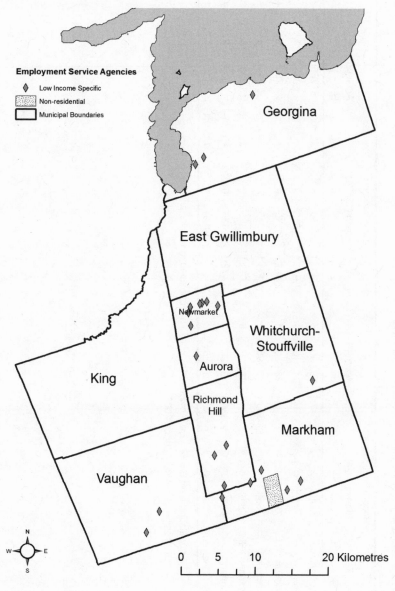

Source: CIVC 2006

Table 5.2 Availability of employment services by municipality

	Recent immigrants						Low-income					
	Youth (15–24)			Adult (25–64)			Youth (15–24)			Adult (25–64)		
	P	S	PS	P	S	PS	P	S	PS	P	S	PS
York Region	18,140	3	6,047:1	68,890	16	4,306:1	17,650	5	3,530:1	57,785	26	2,223:1
Aurora	415	0	–	1,910	1	1,910:1	515	0	–	1,835	1	1,835:1
Markham	7,820	0	–	28,960	4	7,240:1	7,300	0	–	21,760	5	4,352:1
Newmarket	650	1	650:1	2,395	2	1,198:1	945	2	473:1	3,515	8	439:1
Richmond Hill	4,890	0	–	18,105	6	3,018:1	4,385	2	2,193:1	13,285	5	2,657:1
Vaughan	4,070	2	2,035:1	16,435	3	5,478:1	3,435	0	–	13,085	3	4,362:1
Rest of Region	295	0	–	1,085	0	–	1,070	1	1,070:1	4,305	4	1,076:1

Notes: P = population size; S = service providers; PS = ratio of population to service provider

Sources: CIVC 2006; Statistics Canada 2008

youths were also uneven. No services were available for immigrant youths outside Newmarket and Vaughan, and, for low-income youths, outside Newmarket, Richmond Hill, and Georgina.

Accessibility

In low-density suburbs it is not expected that the majority of service users will live within walking distance of a service provider. In fact, travelling to a service location for up to thirty minutes by public transit is considered reasonable. Access to employment service providers was measured using several geospatial methods. According to catchment area analysis, only 1.0 per cent of recent immigrant youths, 6.5 per cent of low-income youths, and 25.3 per cent of the recent immigrant and low-income adults lived within 1.5 kilometres of an employment agency. By comparison, 48.1 per cent of recent immigrant youths, 76.7 per cent of low-income youths, and most of the recent immigrant and low-income adults lived within a thirty-minute bus ride from an employment agency (table 5.3).[1]

In the less urbanized parts of York Region, access to employment services was limited; at most, 16 per cent of the recent immigrants and 33 per cent of the low-income persons in these areas could reach a service provider within a thirty-minute bus ride. For the youth population outside the urbanized core of the region, access was even more limited; less than 4 per cent of recent immigrant youth and 12 per cent of low-income youth were within the thirty-minute transit standard.

While physical access to service is much poorer for recent immigrants and low-income people living in rural areas of York Region than for those in urban areas, access to employment services is also uneven among the urban municipalities. Recent immigrants and low-income people living in Newmarket and Richmond Hill had better access to employment services than did those living in Markham and Vaughan, although these two municipalities housed the largest numbers of recent immigrants and low-income persons. Shortest path analysis also

---

1 These mathematical calculations were based on assumptions of a walking speed of four kilometres an hour along the street network, and a transit speed of thirty kilometres an hour along the transit network. The latter assumption was used because we did not have information on the number of bus transfers and associated waiting time, which depend on bus frequency and are affected by bus delays; however, we assumed that transit riders are informed of the bus schedules and hence calculate their start time accordingly.

Table 5.3 Per cent of population residing in catchment areas of employment service providers, 2006

| | Recent immigrant | | | | | | Low-income | | | | | |
| | Youth (15–24) | | | Adult (25–64) | | | Youth (15–24) | | | Adult (25–64) | | |
	Pop. share	1.5 km walk	30 min. transit	Pop. share	1.5 km walk	30 min. transit	Pop. share	1.5 km walk	30 min. transit	Pop. share	1.5 km walk	30 min. transit
York Region	100.0	1.0	48.1	100.0	24.1	96.5	100.0	6.5	76.7	100.0	25.3	93.7
Aurora	2.3	0.0	97.6	2.8	23.1	99.2	2.9	0.4	98.4	3.2	35.9	99.3
Markham	43.1	0.0	18.5	42.0	14.0	95.4	41.4	0.0	72.0	37.7	22.0	97.0
Newmarket	3.6	20.3	100.0	3.5	40.9	100.0	5.4	48.6	100.0	6.1	74.5	100.0
Richmond Hill	27.0	0.0	45.8	26.3	50.0	100.0	24.8	15.4	100.0	23.0	37.6	100.0
Vaughan	22.4	1.0	97.8	23.9	12.6	99.3	19.5	0.0	67.4	22.6	5.7	99.2
Rest of York Region	1.6	0.0	3.7	1.6	0.0	15.6	6.1	1.0	11.9	7.5	18.9	33.0

Notes: The catchment populations were calculated assuming 4 km/h walking along street network or 30 km/h bussing along transit network

Sources: Statistics Canada 2008; CIVC 2006

showed that it would take a recent immigrant in Newmarket and Richmond Hill less than forty-five minutes to walk to the nearest employment agency, while a recent immigrant living in Vaughan would spend eighty-two minutes, and one living in rural York Region would spend close to five hours (see table 5.4).

For low-income people living in the urbanized municipalities, the picture was similar to that for recent immigrants. However, for those in rural areas, it would take less time walking (101 minutes, compared to 282 minutes for recent immigrants) and more time travelling by transit (86 minutes, compared to 58 minutes for recent immigrants) as a result of the variations in the distribution of low-income people and the availability of employment services within York Region; for example, there were more low-income persons than recent immigrants in Georgina, and accordingly more employment services for the low-income group in general than for recent immigrants specifically.

Finally, accessibility can be gauged by an index that measures the travel distance or travel time between where the vulnerable populations live and where all possible service providers are located. The index shows how easily residents in a neighbourhood can reach services. The larger the index, the greater the ease with which recent immigrants and low-income individuals can access employment services. Each set of indices, pertaining to a travel mode by a vulnerable population group, illustrates the relative accessibility of employment services among different municipalities.

The accessibility indices as shown in table 5.5 confirm the general findings from the catchment area analysis and the shortest path analysis. In general, access to employment services is highest for residents of Newmarket and Richmond Hill, and much lower for those in Vaughan, Markham, and rural York Region. These geographical inequities result most likely from rapid population growth in the southern half of the region where investment in infrastructure has not kept pace. In rural York Region the population is considered too small to support additional investment in infrastructure of all types. In addition, employment services are more accessible for low-income people than for recent immigrants (table 5.5). The high proportion of recent immigrants who have settled in Vaughan and Markham, where employment services are least accessible, exacerbates their access to these essential services. Given the spatial and social inequalities in access, perhaps it is not surprising that Vaughan, Markham, and Georgina also have large numbers of low-income people.

Table 5.4　Average travel time to the closest employment service provider in York Region, 2006 (minutes)

	Recent immigrant			Low-income		
	Service providers	Walk	Transit	Service providers	Walk	Transit
York Region	16	62	19	26	63	24
Aurora	1	49	18	1	43	17
Markham	4	60	18	5	64	21
Newmarket	2	37	14	8	24	10
Richmond Hill	6	40	15	5	43	13
Vaughan	3	82	23	3	84	23
Rest of York Region	0	282	58	4	101	86

Notes: (1) The calculations assumed walking along street network at 4 km/h or travelling by public transit at 30 km/h.
(2) The average travel time is weighted by population in each neighbourhood (or census tract).
Sources: Statistics Canada 2008; CIVC 2006

Awareness of, Use of, and Satisfaction with Employment Services

The survey undertaken for this study asked two questions to probe whether respondents used employment services: "Have you ever used the X services provided by Y?" or "In the last five years, have you used the X services provided by Y?" in which X refers to a type of service, and Y is the name of a service provider. The former applied to employment services for paid workers and the self-employed, and the latter applied to employment services used by the unemployed and those not in the labour force at the time of the survey. In addition to some specifically named service providers, the survey contained for each service type a catch-all question such as, "Have you ever used any other employment services in York Region?" A respondent who said yes to any service provider is deemed a user of employment services.

Employment services were the most heavily used of all social services in this study, although the total number of respondents who used them was relatively small, 258 out of 1,546. The numbers of participants designated as either self-employed ($N = 7$) or unemployed ($N = 43$) were too low to provide a meaningful basis for detailed analysis of their

Table 5.5 Accessibility to employment service providers (SP) in York Region, 2006

| | Recent immigrant | | | | | | Low-income | | | | | |
| | Youth (15–24) | | | Adult (25–64) | | | Youth (15–24) | | | Adult (25–64) | | |
	# SP	Walk	Transit	# SP	Walk	Transit	# SP	Walk	Transit	# SP	Walk	Transit
York Region	3	27	46	16	657	532	5	96	176	26	860	813
Aurora	0	13	14	1	309	390	0	146	135	1	600	573
Markham	0	0	0	4	537	506	0	35	34	5	563	512
Newmarket	1	253	237	2	742	620	2	650	557	8	2,783	2,523
Richmond Hill	0	2	2	6	1,314	1,351	2	590	554	5	1,719	1,738
Vaughan	2	76	97	3	214	218	0	5	4	3	237	276
Rest of York Region	0	0	1	0	2	2	1	27	31	4	144	98

Notes: (1) The calculations assumed walking at 4 km/h along street network or travelling by public transit at 30 km/h.
(2) The weighted accessibility measure is weighted by population in each neighbourhood (or census tract).
Sources: Statistics Canada 2008; CIVC 2006

awareness and use of and satisfaction with employment services. Thus, users of any employment service were grouped together for analysis.

Characteristics of Users and Non-users of Employment Services

Users of employment services did not necessarily belong to the three vulnerable groups in this study. Of the 258 users of employment services in the survey, 124 (48 per cent) were recent immigrants, 54 (21 per cent) had low incomes, and 2 were over sixty-five years of age. As shown in table 5.6, the remaining 78 could have been either Canadian-born individuals or established immigrants who did not have (or no longer had) low incomes or did not want to report their personal and/or household income status.

Table 5.7 indicates that immigrants were more likely to be users of employment services (81 per cent) than to be non-users (76 per cent). Moreover, a larger proportion of immigrants that used employment services were more likely (58 per cent) than the non-users (42 per cent) to have recently arrived to York Region. Consistent with this finding, users were also more likely to speak a language other than English at home (65 per cent) than were the non-users (60 per cent). However, users of employment services were more likely to report Canadian, British, or European ethnic identities (50 per cent) than were the non-users (46 per cent).

The analysis finds that users of employment services tend to have higher levels of formal education than do non-users: 54 per cent of users and 39 per cent of non-users reported that they had a bachelor degree or higher qualifications. With household income, it is noted that somewhat higher proportions of non-users (20 per cent) than users (13 per cent) refused to report their household income. Of those who did report household incomes, a higher proportion of users (31.5 per cent) than non-users (23.9 per cent) reported incomes of $30,000 or less, and a significantly higher proportion of non-users (31.7 per cent) than users (18.6 per cent) reported household incomes of more than $100,000. These differences are likely attributable to the higher number of recent immigrants among users of employment services. Also consistent with the greater numbers of immigrants and recent immigrants among users of employment services is the fact that users were more likely to have lived in York Region for a relatively short period of time (average 7.7 years) compared with non-users of employment services (average 9.5 years).

Table 5.6 Users and non-users of employment services

		Users of employment services				Non-users of employment services	Total
		Recent immigrants	Low-income	Seniors	Other		
Population subgroups	Recent immigrants	90	33	1		416	540
	Low-income	33	–		21	160	214
	Seniors	1		–		234	235
	Other		21	1	57	478	557
Total		124	54	2	78	1,288	1,546

Notes: These figures should be interpreted with caution. Low-income was identified from those who reported either personal or household income. Since a high proportion of respondents did not report their income status, it is likely the total number of low-income people is higher than 54 and that the number of the "other" category is smaller.
Source: Authors' Survey 2008

Table 5.7 Profile of all employment services users and non-users in York Region

	% Users (N = 258)	% Non-users (N = 1,288)
Immigrant	81.0	76.0
Recent immigrant	58.0	42.0
Speaking language other than English at home	65.0	60.0
With BA or higher	54.0	39.0
Canadian, British, or European ethnic identity	50.4	46.1
Refusing to report household income	13.0	19.7
Reporting household income of $30,000 or less	31.5	23.9
Reporting household income of $100,000 or more	18.6	31.7
Average number of years living in York Region	7.8	9.5

Source: Authors' Survey 2008

Recent immigrants, as members of the largest identifiable vulnerable group that uses employment services, deserve more attention. Table 5.8 compares their user and non-user characteristics. Users were, on average, four to five years younger than the non-users. Two-thirds of the users were university educated, compared to less than half of the non-users. In terms of immigration class, users were more likely to be independent skilled migrants, whereas non-users were more likely to be family-class or business-class migrants. Reflecting the immigration patterns of the last three to four decades when immigrants increasingly came from non-traditional or non-European countries, Asians made up the majority of users and non-users. However, immigrants of European backgrounds were more inclined to use employment services.

Recent-immigrant users of employment services were especially vulnerable. Of 124 such individuals, 83 per cent came from non-European countries, and 92 per cent did not speak English at all at home. While two-thirds had at least one university degree, 27 per cent of them lived in households with annual incomes below $30,000 and hence could be classified as low income.

Employment Status of Recent Immigrants

Of the 540 recent-immigrant survey respondents, 31 per cent (n = 165) were not in the labour force at the time of the survey. The proportion of unemployed individuals, 22 per cent (n = 118), was high. About 20 (3 per cent) people did not know how to describe their current employment status or refused to answer the question, 203 (38 per cent) were in paid employment, and 38 (7 per cent) in self-employment. Of those in paid employment, 143 (70 per cent worked full time, 54 (27 per cent) worked part time, and only a few undertook more than one job. The latter and the self-employed likely were those who worked between forty and seventy hours per week, when the median number of hours worked was forty.

Table 5.9 shows how those in paid employment found their current job. While almost 50 per cent found their jobs through conventional means such as job advertisements and personal initiatives (presumably the "other" category in the table), the role of social capital and social agency in immigrant employment needs to be emphasized. The fact that 36 per cent obtained information from friends, families, and co-workers shows the importance of social networks. Moreover, 12 per cent located their jobs through placement services, employment services, or community organizations.

Table 5.8   Profile of recent immigrants using and not using employment services

	% Users (N = 124)	% Non-users (N = 416)
Female	62.9	64.4
Independent-class immigrants	38.9	21.3
Family-class immigrants	34.3	43.3
Business-class immigrants	7.4	16.6
Speaking language other than English at home	91.9	88.9
With BA or higher	67.7	48.8
Non-European ethnic identity	83.1	91.6
Reporting household income of $30,000 or less	27.4	23.8
Using other (non-employment) services	44.4	34.6

Source: Authors' Survey 2008

The survey did not allow us to determine the skill level or the quality of these jobs, but it did ask about the respondents' satisfaction with their jobs. Only 25 per cent were very satisfied with their job, the majority (56 per cent) were somewhat satisfied, and 14 per cent (twenty-eight respondents) were not at all satisfied. Dissatisfaction arose primarily because they were not practising their own profession (six or 21 per cent), the jobs were not challenging (four or 14 per cent) or secure (two or 7 per cent), the pay was low (eight or 29 per cent), or the boss was demanding (five or 18 per cent). These findings suggest that some of the recent-immigrant respondents were under-employed (this, indeed, was confirmed by sixty-six or a third of those having a paid job) and likely considered their jobs to be survival jobs. These latter two reasons for dissatisfaction also have been much cited by those in self-employment as causes for starting their own business (for example, Lo, Teixeira, and Truelove 2002).

A third of those in paid employment did not encounter any problems when they first started searching for their current job. Another half encountered at least one area of difficulty (see table 5.10). These included lack of Canadian work experience (27 per cent), non-recognition of academic or professional credentials (22 per cent), poor language skills (34 per cent), and discrimination (10 per cent). Other difficulties included not knowing where or how to search (21 per cent), and résumés not being prepared according to Canadian expectations (8 per cent).

Table 5.9   Source of information for current job

Source of information	Number	Per cent
Job advertisement in newspaper, Internet, etc.	46	27.1
Friends or acquaintances	44	25.9
Family member or relative	15	8.8
Employment service agency	11	6.5
Placement or job bank agency	4	2.4
Community agency, organization, or association	4	2.4
Co-worker	2	1.2
Promoted	1	0.6
Other	36	21.2
Don't know	6	3.5
Refused	1	0.6
Total	170	100.0

Source: Authors' Survey 2008

The unemployed cited similar challenges in their job-search process but placed more emphasis on the effects of discrimination and on the lack of Canadian work experience. The difficulties cited by the employed and unemployed point to the challenges of ensuring that potential workers have the experience, skills, and language fluency that employers need, and of educating employers about recent immigrants' experience and skills. Some difficulties, such as non-familiarity with the search process in particular, point to the continuing need for employment services to integrate newcomers successfully into the labour market.

Recent-Immigrants' Use of Employment Services

The 124 recent immigrants who had used employment services comprised 56 per cent (sixty-nine) in paid employment, 2 per cent (two) in self-employment, 26 per cent (thirty-two) unemployed, and 17 per cent (twenty-one) of the other groups who were not actively working or seeking jobs at the time of the survey (for example, retirees, students, homemakers, and those on disability benefits).

Table 5.11 lists the employment service providers named in the survey and shows that the use of employment services by recent

Table 5.10   Difficulties encountered in job search

	By paid employees (N = 170)*		By the unemployed (N = 116)*	
	N	%	N	%
Total encountering difficulties	83	49.0	52	45.0
None of the following, but not specified	23	27.7	20	38.5
English not fluent enough	28	33.7	–	–
Lack of Canadian work experience	22	26.5	16	30.8
Non-familiarity with job-search process	17	20.5	13	25.0
Academic or professional credentials not recognized	18	21.7	7	13.5
Few job openings in respondent's field	9	10.8	–	–
Résumé not in a Canadian style	7	8.4	–	–
Was refused employment owing to age, skin colour, cultural background, accent ...	8	9.6	20	38.5
Lack of computer or other skills required by the job	7	8.4	6	11.5
No formal schooling	1	1.2	–	–
Jobs too far away	–	–	3	5.8
Unhelpful employment services	–	–	5	9.6

* Excluding those who said that they did not encounter any difficulties.
Source: Authors' Survey 2008

immigrants did not vary between the two samples described in chapter 3, that is, the random sample chosen for a telephone interview, and the purposeful sample made up of respondents recommended by service providers. Users of employment services made up 23.4 per cent of the random sample and 22.7 per cent of the purposeful sample. More people from the random sample accessed employment services provided by Agency A (76 per cent of service users) and Agency B (28 per cent of service users), whereas more people from the purposeful sample used Agency C (67 per cent of service users) and Agency D (29 per cent of service users) – a difference likely caused by the active recruitment of respondents for the purposeful sample by agencies C and D.

Some respondents were unable to get help with services that could enhance their employment and self-employment opportunities. They

Table 5.11 Use of employment services by recent immigrants

	Employment status				Sample		
	Self-employed	Paid workers	Un-employed	Other	Total	Random	Purposeful
Recent immigrants	38	203	118	165	540*	231	309
Service users	2	69	32	21	124	54	70
Employment Agency:							
Agency A		76.8%	28.1%	23.8%	54.9%	75.9%	42.9%
Agency B		31.9%	9.4%	42.9%	27.9%	27.8%	21.4%
Agency C		46.4%	62.5%	14.3%	45.1%	25.9%	67.1%
Agency D		15.9%	32.5%	0	17.2%	7.4%	28.6%
Agency E		4.3%	10.0%	0	4.9%	7.4%	5.7%
Other agencies		11.6%	14.3%	4.29%	17.2%	18.5%	18.6%
Self-employment agency:							
Agency F	50.0%					100.0%	0
Agency G	0					0	0
Agency B	0					0	0
Other agencies	50.0%					0	100.0%

* Including 16 who provided no information on their employment status.
Source: Authors' Survey 2008

included 9 per cent of those in paid work, 16 per cent of those in self-employment, and, more significantly, 21 per cent of the unemployed and 19 per cent of those not in the labour force. Overall, 14 per cent of recent immigrants did not manage to get help with employment and self-employment when they needed it. This is a significant proportion, although the reasons for this problem are not clear.

Satisfaction with Employment Services

During the survey, respondents were asked not only to comment on their use of service agencies but also to indicate, on a four-point scale, their degree of satisfaction with the service provided by each agency

Table 5.12 Satisfaction scores for employment services used, by selected factors

Immigrant status*	Satisfaction score	N
Non-immigrants	1.73	46
Immigrants	2.08	201
Length of immigration**		
Recent immigrants (0–10 years)	2.00	117
Established immigrants (> 10 years)	2.22*	81
Age at immigration**		
10–19	2.23	57
20–30	2.19	59
31–45	1.90	61
46+	1.79	17
Ethnicity*		
British	1.86	17
European	1.70	49
Indian, Asian, and other	2.12	185

* significant at $\alpha = 0.01$, ** significant at $\alpha = 0.1$.
Source: Authors' Survey 2008

they used. Since one person could have multiple responses to a particular service item, a multiple-response procedure was used to calculate a mean satisfaction score. The mean satisfaction scores – ranging between one and four, with one indicating "very satisfied," and four "very dissatisfied" – were tested against some socio-economic demographic variables. The results are shown in table 5.12.

Overall, the mean satisfaction scores were about two, indicating that low-income people and recent immigrants were generally, though not overwhelmingly, satisfied with the employment services received. Analysing the relationships between socio-economic and demographic variables and satisfaction with services showed some statistically significant relationships. Table 5.12 reveals that only immigrant status and ethnic identity are related to satisfaction with employment services; age at which the respondent immigrated to Canada and time since the respondent immigrated to Canada exhibit weak and insignificant relationships.

Immigrants were significantly less likely than non-immigrants to be satisfied with the employment services they used in York Region. Nevertheless, recent immigrants were more satisfied than established immigrants with any employment services they used; their mean satisfaction score, at below two, indicated that they were somewhat satisfied with the employment services they used. This finding is not consistent with the literature on the difficulties that recent immigrants have experienced in accessing the labour market, although the difference in mean score between that of recent and of established immigrants was only slightly significant. One possible explanation is that immigrants arriving in the last decade, compared with those arriving in earlier decades (that is, the 1980s and the first half of the 1990s), were more aware of the difficulties they were going to face in the Canadian labour market, had lower expectations, and regarded as useful any services leading to positive employment outcomes.

Table 5.12 also shows that among those who immigrated to Canada satisfaction with employment services tends to be positively related to the age at arrival, with those arriving at older ages being more generally satisfied with any employment services used. In addition, respondents with non-British and non-European ethnic identities were significantly less likely to express general satisfaction with the employment services. This finding is consistent with reports that visible-minority immigrants experience more hardships in the labour market.

Further analysis indicated some relationship between length of residence in York Region, time spent as immigrants in Canada, and satisfaction with employment services. For recent immigrants, that is, those who migrated to Canada within the last ten years, there was no relationship between satisfaction with employment services and being very new or new to the region, beginning to establish oneself (four to five years), being established (six to ten years), and being well established (in excess of ten years). However, for immigrants who had lived in Canada for more than ten years, there were significant contrasts between the "beginning-to-establish-oneself" group and the other groups of non-recent immigrants who had lived in York Region for either fewer years or more years. For reasons not immediately identifiable, those in the "beginning-to-establish-oneself" group (that is, those who had moved to the region in around 2003) were significantly less satisfied with the employment services used than were the non-recent immigrants in all other groups. This finding warrants further analyses.

Summary and Conclusions

Analysis of employment shows, in stark relief, the impact of neoliberalism on the outer suburbs. Despite its popular reputation as a region of wealth and affluence, York Region is home to growing numbers of recent immigrants and low-income persons who experience low labour-force-participation rates and high unemployment rates. Although the retirement of an aging population contributes to low incomes, underemployment and unemployment play a not insignificant role, particularly for recent immigrants. Over a quarter of the low-income population in York Region and over half of the low-income respondents in the survey are recent immigrants who struggle to earn wages commensurate with their qualifications and experience (Picot 2008). The traditional patterns of economic outcomes for recent immigrants are altering, and not for the better. The earnings gap during the first few years in Canada between immigrants and the Canadian-born has been increasing, in spite of the rising educational attainment of immigrants. The incidence of low incomes among successive cohorts of new immigrants has also been rising (Picot 2008).

The analyses confirm that recent immigrants in York Region are disproportionately engaged in the precarious forms of employment that heighten economic inequality. In this context, access to and use of employment service agencies are important for ensuring successful settlement and integration. Employment services in York Region are, however, unevenly distributed. Recent immigrants and low-income people living in Newmarket and Richmond Hill have better access to employment services than do their counterparts residing in Markham and Vaughan. This is a particularly disturbing finding because the latter two municipalities have the largest numbers of recent immigrants and low-income persons.

The potential benefits of this type of social infrastructure, employment services, are also reduced by the residents' lack of awareness and use of available services. Only a small percentage of people in the region have used employment services. Many recent immigrants who settle in York Region may be unaware that social services are available especially if such services are not available in their country of origin. The lack of knowledge that employment services exist can make the settlement process for newcomers very challenging and stressful, especially if they do not speak English and they arrive with limited financial resources. Survey results from this study indicate the importance of conducting further research with respect to vulnerable populations who are unaware of employment services and do not use such services. Do non-users rely on alternative strategies for locating jobs? If so, what strategies do they use and with what outcomes?

"There is a need for stronger communication and outreach to newcomers about the existence of such services, who are entitled to use services, and how to access them" (Lo et al. 2007, 79). Outreach through alternative media such as videotapes and Internet sites and targeted media campaigns, and outreach to community organizations serving recent immigrants and low-income households are needed to ensure that all vulnerable individuals are aware that there are services into which they can tap.

Both the census and the survey reveal that high proportions of recent immigrants and low-income individuals rely on public transit to travel in the region. A geographical mismatch may well be one reason for the limited use of employment services. For low-income residents the expenses incurred in using public transit to reach employment agencies may act as an access barrier, particularly when trips across regions require payment of several fares. York Region should explore the introduction of subsidies to support the use of public transit by low-income individuals for the purpose of reaching employment service providers, in a way similar to the one-year pilot project in place at the time of this study, whose purpose was to supply discounted transit fares to community-based agencies serving the homeless (York Regional Council Meeting 2008). It will help to remove an important barrier to obtaining help from social service agencies.

The analysis of employment services illustrates the potential as well as the limits of social infrastructure to address the inequalities associated with contemporary neoliberalism. While employment services are a form of social infrastructure intended to help low-income residents and recent immigrants to avoid the underemployment and unemployment from which economic inequality derives, in York Region few low-income residents and recent immigrants are aware of or use available services. A geographical mismatch, compounded by costly and slow public transit, certainly contributes to low rates of awareness and use. However, more effective means of advertising the services and informing people about their utility are also necessary. This is a difficult task in the current neoliberal context where the emphasis on individual responsibility discourages people from expecting and seeking assistance.

6 Housing Infrastructure in York Region

Introduction

Affordable, adequate, and suitable housing is an essential prerequisite for a successful life in Canada (Hulchanski and Shapcott 2004; Preston et al. 2009). At the national, provincial, and metropolitan levels several studies have highlighted affordability as the main housing issue facing Canadians (Engeland and Lewis 2005; Prentice 2009). Within Canadian cities little attention has been paid to housing in the outer suburbs, where two major social trends collide. The housing stock consists almost exclusively of expensive, single-family, detached, and owner-occupied housing (Bunting et al. 2004; Suttor 2007) while the rapidly increasing population is growing more diverse. Recent immigrants are settling directly in the inner and outer suburbs of Canada's largest metropolitan areas (Murdie 2008); the number of seniors is increasing, as is the number of low-income households. While the three populations are growing rapidly in the outer suburbs, the housing suitable for each group remains in short supply. To illustrate the current challenges this chapter examines the housing circumstances for each of the three vulnerable populations in York Region: people in low-income households, recent immigrants, and seniors. The suitability of housing is assessed through an evaluation of household size; however, the analysis emphasizes housing affordability for two reasons. As has been stated, affordability is the main housing issue for Canadians, particularly recent immigrants and low-income households (Preston et al. 2009). Information about affordability is also readily available, unlike information about suitability and adequacy.[1] With the data compiled for this study, the housing demand from each group was assessed, the affordability and the suitability of current housing were evaluated, the geographical match between supply and demand for each vulnerable group was ascertained, and each group's use of and satisfaction with housing services was examined.

Assessment of Demand

The three vulnerable groups – recent immigrants, people with low incomes, and seniors – accounted for approximately 250,000 York Region residents in 2006. They included 109,275 recent immigrants, 112,165 people with low incomes, and 87,620 seniors (table 3.1). Reflecting the rapid population growth in the region thanks to an influx of working-age adults and their families, the number of seniors was lower than the numbers of other vulnerable groups.

To estimate the housing demand of each group, it is important to remember that the three vulnerable groups overlap (table 3.1). The intersection of the three dimensions of vulnerability often compounds the difficulties of obtaining affordable, adequate, and suitable housing. The analysis concentrates on household characteristics because households are the basic unit of housing demand. Three factors – household size, household composition, and household income – are major determinants of housing demand. Household size and composition determine the number of rooms required for the household to have suitable housing. Household income is the principal determinant of housing affordability.

Household Size

In York Region, household size varies markedly among the three vulnerable groups (table 6.1). According to the 2006 census, low-income and recent-immigrant households were larger than the regional average. With an average size of 3.9 people, slightly more than half of the low-income households had one more person than the average

---

1 Although the census provides information about adequacy, based on reports of need for major and minor repairs, the information about suitability is difficult to calculate without micro-data describing each housing situation and household composition.

Table 6.1 Housing demand by vulnerable group

	Total population	Low-income	Recent immigrants	Seniors
Average household size	3.2	3.9	4.4	3.0
Median household income	$81,928	$23,478	$67,456	$66,289
Below low- income cut-off (LICO)	12.7%	100.0%	27.1%	12.2%

Source: Statistics Canada 2008

household in York Region (3.2). Recent-immigrant households had, on average, more than one additional person per household. With an average size of 3.0 people, seniors' households were slightly smaller than the average York Region household. One result of these trends is that low-income households and recent immigrants are looking for large dwellings to accommodate their households, while seniors can fit more easily into smaller dwelling units.

Household Income

Household income also varies among the three vulnerable groups. Median household income for low-income households was $23,478 in 2005, less than one-third of the median household income for York Region of $81,928. Such households will have tremendous difficulty locating affordable housing in York Region where in 2005 the average sales price for a single-family house was $477,000.

Recent immigrants and seniors in York Region are better off than people with low incomes, having median household incomes in 2005 of $67,456 and $66,289, respectively. Nevertheless, the median household incomes of the two groups place both at a disadvantage in the York Region housing market. Each group had a median household income that was substantially less than the median for the regional population. With income disparities of $14,472 and $15,639 respectively, recent immigrants and seniors will have difficulty competing in the local housing market. With more than one-quarter of recent immigrants (27.1 per cent) and about one-tenth of seniors (12.2 per cent) having household incomes below the low-income cut-off, housing affordability will be a serious challenge for large numbers of these vulnerable populations.

Household Composition

In addition to household size and household income, household composition often affects the demand for different types and sizes of dwellings and the financial situation of the household. Couples with children often have the means to purchase from the growing supply of single-family detached dwellings with three or four bedrooms. Small households, such as households of unattached persons or those headed by single parents, often have more limited financial resources. Multi-family households that include more than one nuclear family are in a contradictory position. On the one hand, large households need bigger dwellings that are usually more expensive, while on the other hand, as Hiebert and Mendez (2008) have noted, multi-family households can pool their incomes to afford more expensive dwellings. Household composition is a particularly influential factor in the York Region housing market, where the housing supply caters to couples with children; there are a large number of single-family detached dwellings with three or four bedrooms. Small units appropriate for single-parent and single-person households are not as plentiful, while the extra-large units needed by multi-family households are expensive.

Household composition varies across the three vulnerable groups. More than half of all low-income residents in York Region (54.1 per cent) lived in households that consisted of couples with children in 2006 (table 6.2). As indicated elsewhere (Hulchanski and Shapcott 2004), single-parent households accounted for a high percentage of all low-income households (12 per cent). Unattached persons were an equal percentage of the low-income population. The large immigrant population in York Region was reflected in the high percentage of people with low incomes living in multi-family households (20.7 per cent).

Among recent immigrants, 60 per cent were couples with children, the age group targeted by current immigration policies. There were few single parents or unattached persons in this group; however, almost one-third of recent immigrants lived in multi-family households, a trend that has had a significant impact on housing demand in the region. The small households of seniors were reflected in the low percentage of seniors living as couples with children and as single parents, 20.3 per cent and 7.2 per cent, respectively. Many seniors lived alone or in multi-family households.

When household composition and household income are considered together, the challenges for recent immigrants and low-income persons

Table 6.2   Household composition for each vulnerable group

	Couples with children		Single parents		Unattached persons		Multi-family households	
	N	%	N	%	N	%	N	%
Low-income	56,180	54.1	13,410	12.9	12,825	12.3	21,495	20.7
Recent immigrants	61,285	59.4	4,725	4.6	2,780	2.7	33,850	32.8
Seniors	10,920	20.3	3,850	7.2	14,185	26.4	24,870	46.2

Source: Statistics Canada 2008

become readily apparent. Both groups had large households because of the presence of couples with children and, in the case of recent immigrants, multiple families. Yet, on average, recent immigrants had less income to spend on housing because their median household income was below the regional median household income. The contradiction was even more acute for low-income households that have very low median household incomes despite their large household size. By comparison, seniors are likely to experience less difficulty in the York Region housing market. Although their median household income was below the regional median, almost half of them lived in multi-family households where family incomes are likely to be pooled, providing more financial resources for housing for seniors.

Geography of Housing Demand

The uneven geography of housing demand compounds the challenges of locating adequate, suitable, and affordable housing. Each type of household was distributed unevenly across the region (table 6.3). Markham, where the vulnerable populations were most concentrated, was home to the largest percentages of each type of household in 2006. Vaughan and Richmond Hill followed. The remainder of each vulnerable population was distributed among Aurora, Newmarket, and the rest of York Region.

The predominance of recent immigrants in Markham means that it had the largest percentage of recent immigrants living in each type of household (table 6.3), followed by Richmond Hill and Vaughan. Richmond Hill, however, had a larger percentage of the recent immigrant population than did Vaughan, where there is a predominance of

Table 6.3   Household composition by vulnerable group

Low-income	Couples with children	Single parents	Unattached persons	Multi-family households
Total (N)	56,180	13,410	12,825	21,495
Aurora	2.9%	4.9%	5.7%	2.6%
Markham	39.9%	30.4%	24.8%	44.8%
Newmarket	4.1%	11.8%	14.2%	3.5%
Richmond Hill	24.0%	24.7%	20.4%	20.1%
Vaughan	23.8%	18.2%	20.1%	22.7%
Rest of York Region	5.4%	10.1%	14.8%	6.4%
Recent immigrants	Couples with children	Single parents	Unattached persons	Multi-family households
Total (N)	61,285	4,725	2,780	33,850
Aurora	3.6%	2.7%	2.2%	1.5%
Markham	38.4%	43.9%	39.6%	49.0%
Newmarket	4.1%	1.7%	4.0%	2.3%
Richmond Hill	29.0%	30.8%	29.7%	21.4%
Vaughan	23.1%	19.6%	23.2%	24.3%
Rest of York Region	1.8%	1.4%	1.4%	1.5%
Seniors	Couples with children	Single parents	Unattached persons	Multi-family households
Total (N)	10,920	3,850	14,185	24,870
Aurora	4.0%	5.2%	5.9%	2.6%
Markham	33.2%	31.0%	24.5%	40.2%
Newmarket	5.1%	8.2%	12.4%	4.5%
Richmond Hill	16.8%	22.0%	17.7%	21.0%
Vaughan	30.4%	22.6%	19.9%	24.6%
Rest of York Region	10.5%	11.0%	19.6%	7.2%

Source: Statistics Canada 2008

Canadian-born children and grandchildren of immigrants. Relatively few recent immigrants lived in Aurora, Newmarket, or the rest of York Region.

The geographical distributions of household types for people with low incomes and seniors differed slightly from those for recent immigrants. Markham had the largest percentage of low-income people in each household type, while Vaughan and Richmond Hill respectively were home to approximately one-fifth of the low-income people in each type of household. Single parents and unattached individuals who have low incomes were found in substantial numbers in Newmarket and the rest of York Region – municipalities where the small numbers of recent immigrants mean that there are few low-income couples and few multi-family households. Aurora stood out with a small percentage, less than 6 per cent, of the low-income population in any household type.

Although Markham was home to the largest percentage of seniors from each type of household, the aging of the Vaughan population was apparent in the high percentages of seniors from each household type living in the municipality. Approximately 30 per cent of all seniors living as couples with children and another 24.6 per cent living in multi-family households resided in Vaughan. In comparison, only 16.8 per cent of all seniors living as couples with children were in Richmond Hill. The rest of York Region ranks fourth, with almost 20 per cent of seniors in the region living as unattached persons and approximately 10 per cent of those living in households of couples with children and as single parents. According to the 2006 census, Newmarket had a small percentage of seniors, as did Aurora.

The trends in household composition for the three vulnerable groups and their uneven geographical distributions cause housing demand to vary across the region. In Markham there were substantial numbers of each vulnerable group, and large numbers of people from each group living in every type of household. In every other location the demand for housing was limited to only one or two of the vulnerable groups, be they recent immigrants, low-income households, or seniors.

Housing Tenure

Homeownership was the dominant form of tenure for all vulnerable groups in York Region. More than three-quarters of the low-income population (76.4 per cent) lived in owner-occupied housing (table 6.4).

The dominance of ownership was even more marked among recent immigrants and seniors, of whom 87.8 per cent and 90.0 per cent, respectively, were homeowners. The high rates of homeownership in York Region differed from the high rates of renting reported for low-income populations and recent immigrants living in the City of Toronto and other Canadian cities (Engeland and Lewis 2005; Hiebert et al. 2006; Preston et al. 2009). The differences in tenure among the three vulnerable populations in York Region reflected their ability to purchase housing and their eligibility for subsidized rental housing (see table 6.4). Low-income households whose median income was well below the median household income for the region were more likely to qualify for subsidized rental housing than were households from the other two groups.

Geographical variations in housing tenure are complex. For low-income households the percentage living in rental accommodation in 2006 varied from a high of 41.6 per cent in Newmarket to 16.4 per cent in Vaughan (table 6.5). Vaughan and Markham, with the largest low-income populations, also reported the lowest percentages of low-income households who were renting. Although seniors were less likely to rent than people with low incomes, the spatial patterns of seniors who rented were similar to those of renters with low incomes. Newmarket had the highest percentage of seniors who rented, followed by Aurora and the rest of York Region; Vaughan and Markham reported the lowest percentages of seniors who were renters. The uneven geographical patterns of renting by low-income households and seniors seem to reflect the supplies of social housing and assisted housing for seniors. Both types of housing are concentrated in Newmarket and the rest of York Region. For recent immigrants there was little geographical variation in housing tenure, although in the four municipalities designated as the rest of York Region more recent immigrants rented than in any other municipality.

Dwelling Costs

Housing costs were below the regional average for two vulnerable groups: seniors and low-income people (table 6.6). Seniors spent the least on housing, whether they were renters or owners, with an average gross monthly rent of $906, more than $100 less than the average for the region, and an average major monthly payment of $915 for owners, more than $500 below the regional average. The low-income population also had housing costs below the regional average, but here the

Table 6.4   Housing tenure by vulnerable group in York Region

	Total	Low-income	Recent immigrants	Seniors
Total	275,200	112,165	109,275	87,620
Owner	88.3%	76.4%	87.8%	90.0%
Renter	11.7%	23.6%	12.2%	10.0%

Source: Statistics Canada 2008

Table 6.5   Housing tenure by vulnerable group and municipality, 2006

Low-income	Total tenure	% Owner	% Renter
York Region	112,165	76.4	23.6
Aurora	3,825	66.9	32.9
Markham	41,880	78.5	21.4
Newmarket	7,175	58.3	41.6
Richmond Hill	25,570	75.1	24.8
Vaughan	25,270	83.7	16.4
Rest of York Region	8,455	67.9	32.0
Recent immigrants	Total tenure	% Owner	% Renter
York Region	109,275	87.8	12.2
Aurora	3,070	87.1	13.2
Markham	45,805	86.0	14.0
Newmarket	3,820	88.7	11.0
Richmond Hill	29,135	89.0	11.1
Vaughan	25,490	89.9	10.0
Rest of York Region	1,955	81.6	16.1
Seniors	Total tenure	% Owner	% Renter
York Region	87,620	90.0	10.0
Aurora	3,715	84.7	15.3
Markham	26,930	90.8	9.0
Newmarket	6,445	82.6	17.2
Richmond Hill	15,630	88.5	11.4
Vaughan	22,415	93.9	6.3
Rest of York Region	12,485	88.3	11.7

Source: Statistics Canada 2008

Table 6.6 Housing costs by vulnerable group, 2005

	Total	Low-income	Recent immigrants	Seniors
Average gross monthly rent	$1,042	$893	$1,057	$906
Average owner major monthly payments	$1,490	$1,395	$1,830	$915

Source: Statistics Canada 2008

difference in average monthly costs was more pronounced for renters than for homeowners. Gross rent was $149 less per month for the average low-income renter, whereas major payments were $95 less per month for low-income owners.

Recent immigrants entered the housing market in the past ten years as housing costs escalated steadily, and they paid higher housing costs than did either of the other two vulnerable groups. Recent immigrants also paid higher rents and higher ownership costs than did the average person in the region. Their average gross rent of $1,057 was marginally higher than the regional average of $1,042. Recent immigrants who were homeowners paid a much higher premium – an additional $340 per month – than did the average homeowner in the region.

Housing Affordability

The impact of high housing costs was apparent in two measures of housing affordability developed by the Canada Mortgage and Housing Corporation. According to CMHC, households experience financial strain when they spend 30 per cent or more of their total before-tax income on average monthly rent or average owner's major monthly payments. Serious financial distress occurs when households spend 50 per cent or more of their total before-tax income on housing (Hulchanski and Shapcott 2005).

HOUSING AFFORDABILITY BY VULNERABLE GROUP
Of the three vulnerable groups the low-income individuals reported the highest levels of financial strain and financial distress. Of the 112,165 low-income individuals in York Region in 2006, 80.8 per cent spent at least 30 per cent of their total income before taxes on housing, and 62.6 per cent spent at least 50 per cent of their total income on housing (table 6.7). Housing-affordability problems were less pronounced for

recent immigrants, although the numbers reporting affordability problems still were substantial. Of the 109,275 recent immigrants living in York Region, 46.7 per cent spent at least 30 per cent of their household income on housing, and another 25.4 per cent spent at least 50 per cent of their household income on housing (compared with proportions of 26.0 per cent and 12.0 per cent, respectively, for the total population). Seniors were the least likely of the three populations to have affordability problems. With low average rents and low monthly major payments, less than one in four seniors was spending 30 per cent or more of their total before-tax income on housing, and only 8.5 per cent were spending 50 per cent or more of their total income on housing (table 6.7).

GEOGRAPHIES OF HOUSING AFFORDABILITY

Uneven geographies of housing affordability characterize York Region, where each vulnerable group has a different spatial pattern of housing affordability. For the low-income population, in which approximately 80 per cent of the population is spending at least 30 per cent of total gross income on housing, housing affordability was an issue throughout the region (figure 6.1). In 142 of the 154 census tracts in the region at least half of the low-income population was spending 30 per cent or more of its total before-tax income on housing.

Fewer low-income households were experiencing serious financial distress by paying more than 50 per cent of their income on housing, but, again, these households were widely distributed. In 135 census tracts at least half of the low-income population was spending 50 per cent or more of total before-tax income on housing. Severe affordability problems, where more than three-quarters of the low-income population were spending at least 50 per cent of total before-tax income on housing, were spatially concentrated in Whitchurch-Stouffville, Richmond Hill, the northern half of Markham, and the southern half of Newmarket.

Housing affordability was a problem for many recent immigrants, but it was less prevalent and less widespread for recent immigrants than for people with low incomes. As mentioned earlier, a smaller percentage of recent immigrants than of people with low incomes reported affordability problems. In 56 of the 154 census tracts in the region at least half of recent immigrants spent 30 per cent or more of total before-tax income on housing (figure 6.2). This number of census tracts is much smaller than the number for the low-income population. There

Table 6.7   Housing affordability by vulnerable group, 2005

	Total population	Low-income	Recent immigrants	Seniors
Spending > 30%	26.0%	80.8%	46.7%	22.6%
Spending > 50%	12.0%	62.6%	25.4%	8.5%

Source: Statistics Canada 2008

were only seven census tracts where half of the recent immigrants were spending at least 50 per cent of total before-tax income on housing. Again, this is a much smaller number than for the low-income population.

For recent immigrants, housing-affordability problems were concentrated in the southern half of the region and in Newmarket. Certain census tracts in Aurora, King, and Whitchurch-Stouffville (figure 6.2) also had high proportions of recent immigrants who were experiencing housing-affordability problems. Census tracts in which more than half of recent immigrants were spending 30 per cent or more of total before-tax income on housing were concentrated in Richmond Hill, Markham, and Vaughan, municipalities in which the recent immigrant population was concentrated. The same was true for the census tracts in which more than one-quarter of recent immigrants were spending 50 per cent or more of total before-tax income on housing.

Of the three vulnerable groups, seniors were the least likely to report housing-affordability problems, a finding reflected in the geographical distribution of affordability. More than one-quarter of seniors spent 30 per cent or more of total before-tax income on housing in only 47 of the 154 census tracts (figure 6.3). The percentage of seniors reporting housing-affordability problems did not exceed 40 per cent of the senior population in any census tract. Indeed, there was no census tract in 2005 in which the percentage of seniors spending half or more of total before-tax income on housing exceeded 19 per cent.

The spatial distributions underscore the relatively limited housing-affordability problems for seniors. The majority of the census tracts in which at least one-quarter of seniors were spending 30 per cent or more of total before-tax income on housing were concentrated in the southern half of the region, along with selected tracts in Newmarket and Whitchurch-Stouffville. The distribution of census tracts where at least one in eight seniors was experiencing serious affordability problems

Figure 6.1   Housing affordability for the low-income population in York Region, 2005

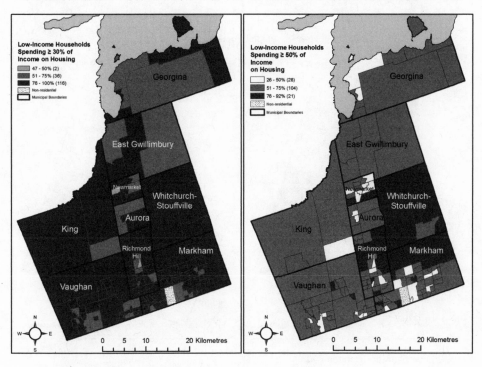

Source: Statistics Canada 2008

was sparse, with the majority found in Markham and Richmond Hill. In a few tracts in Vaughan, King, and Newmarket, at least 12.6 per cent of seniors were spending 50 per cent or more of total before-tax income on housing. Clearly, of the three vulnerable groups under consideration, seniors were the least likely to be struggling with housing affordability.

Geography of Social and Assisted-Living Housing

In 2006, social housing, in which rents are subsidized, and assisted housing, which serves frail seniors by providing meals, caretaking, and

Figure 6.2   Housing affordability for recent immigrants in York Region, 2005

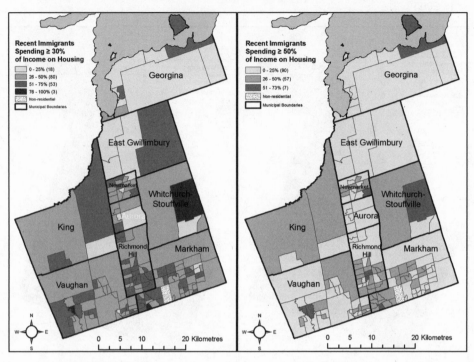

Source: Statistics Canada 2008

some nursing as well as shelter, were distributed unevenly across York Region.[2] The majority of social housing was located in Newmarket, Aurora, and Richmond Hill (figure 6.4). Some was found in Markham and Vaughan, but there were fewer developments and the developments were smaller in these two municipalities. Figure 6.4 indicates how the provision of social housing has changed over time. Municipally owned and operated public housing, which was built mainly in the 1970s, was concentrated in Newmarket, an important regional centre distant from the City of Toronto at the time that most public housing was built. Cooperative and non-profit housing, which were promoted

_____

2 *Independent living for seniors* refers to social housing for seniors.

Figure 6.3 Housing affordability for seniors in York Region, 2005

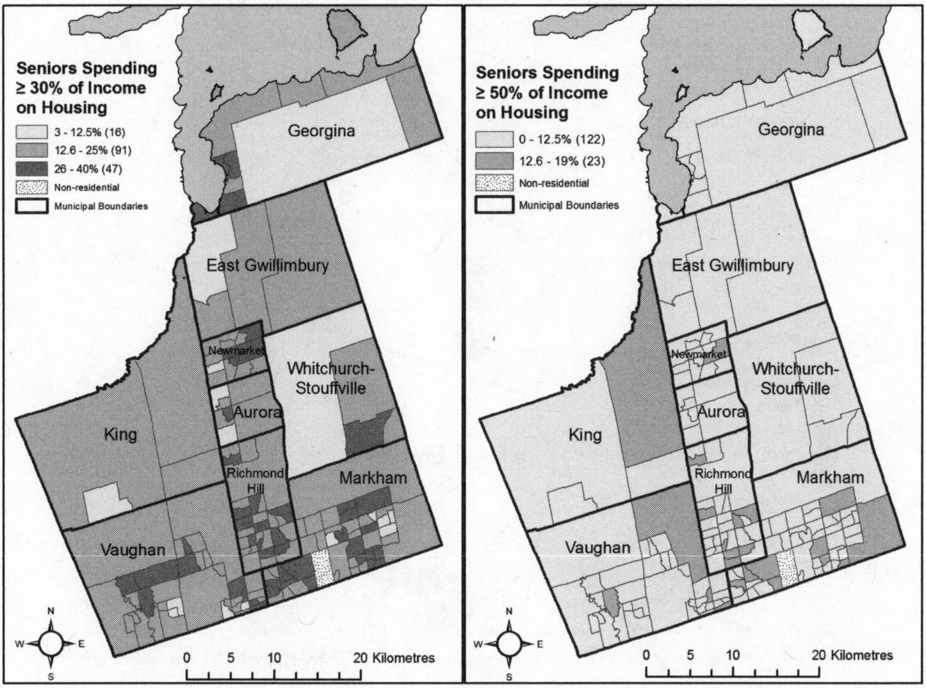

Source: Statistics Canada 2008

in the 1980s and early 1990s, were located in the municipalities to the south – Aurora, Richmond Hill, Markham, and Vaughan – where development accelerated in those decades (Hackworth 2008; Hackworth and Moriah 2006). Since 2000, renewed interest in the provision of social housing by both the federal and the provincial government has resulted in the addition of cooperative and non-profit housing units in the southern part of York Region, where the population is concentrated. However, as in the rest of Ontario, the number of additional units is small (Hackworth 2008).

The location of social housing in York Region affects access to social infrastructure for the minority of vulnerable residents who benefit from affordable housing. Concentrated along Yonge Street, much of

Figure 6.4   Distribution of social housing in York Region, 2006

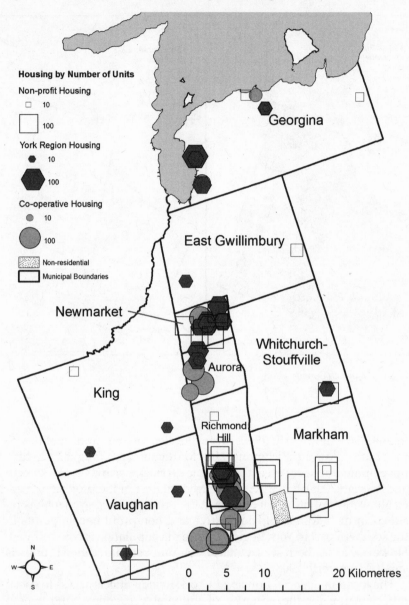

Source: Statistics Canada 2008; CIVC 2006

the current social-housing stock, particularly the non-profit and cooperative housing, is located near public transit that runs frequently along
this major north–south artery. In contrast, several municipal public
housing developments are located in distant northern locations and
the western half of the region where public transportation is sparse
and slow. In Markham and Vaughan, several non-profit and cooperative housing developments are also far from major arteries with better
transit service. Proximity to transit services enhances access to all other
forms of social infrastructure for individuals from the three vulnerable
groups. This is particularly true for settlement, employment, and adult
educational services that are fairly concentrated within the region.
Nearby transit has less impact on access to the publicly funded educational facilities for children that are widely dispersed throughout York
Region.

Unlike social housing, the assisted-living facilities for seniors were
roughly proportional to the population in each municipality, with the
exception of Vaughan where there were only four locations (table 6.8).
Social housing for seniors, identified as independent-living developments, was distributed unevenly, with concentrations in Newmarket,
Richmond Hill, and the rest of York Region. The shortage of housing
for seniors in Vaughan is noteworthy because of its large senior
population.

In the same way, social housing for low-income residents was not
distributed proportionately among municipalities. For example, 6 per
cent of the region's low-income population lived in Newmarket, where
24 per cent of social housing for low-income residents was located. In
contrast, in Vaughan, where 22.5 per cent of the low-income population
in York Region lived, we find only 14.5 per cent of the region's low-
income social housing stock. The population served by each housing
provider varied across the region. Newmarket emerged as the best-
served municipality, in which the numbers of seniors and low-income
people per housing provider were lower than the ratio of the population per housing provider for the entire region (table 6.9). Aurora and
Richmond Hill also had lower populations per social housing provider
for seniors and for the low-income population. In both cases, as figure
6.4 shows, there were several social housing providers, and the senior
and low-income populations were small. Markham and Vaughan stood
out as the municipalities in which the supplies of social housing were
inadequate in relation to their senior and low-income populations.

Table 6.8 Housing for seniors and low-income populations

	Seniors assisted living*	Seniors independent living**	Low-income
York Region	26	57	62
Aurora	1	3	4
Markham	8	9	11
Newmarket	6	10	15
Richmond Hill	4	14	16
Vaughan	4	7	9
Rest of York Region	3	14	7

* Retirement homes.
** Social housing, life-lease housing, and housing help centres.
Source: CIVC 2006

Table 6.9 Population per housing provider, York Region, 2006

	Seniors assisted living	Seniors independent living	Low-income
York Region	3,533	1,612	1,808
Aurora	4,230	1,410	957
Markham	3,481	3,094	3,803
Newmarket	1,179	708	478
Richmond Hill	4,096	1,170	1,596
Vaughan	5,820	3,326	2,809
Rest of York Region	4,350	4,350	1,206

Source: CIVC 2006

Use of Social, Assisted-Living, and Independent-Living Housing and Other Housing Services

The limited supply of social housing for seniors and low-income residents and the limited number of locations offering assisted-living housing for seniors mean that only 76 of the 1,546 respondents who participated in the survey had lived in social housing or assisted-living housing or used any housing services.[3] Owing to their small numbers, it was not possible to distinguish users of specific types of housing and specific services, so the analysis in this chapter aggregated all forms of subsidized housing – public, non-profit, and cooperative housing and assisted-living housing – and services such as housing information centres and legal aid with landlord-tenant disputes. Despite the small number of users, a comparison of their social characteristics with those of non-users provided information about the housing needs that were being met and those that deserved more attention.

Residents of social housing and assisted-living housing for seniors and users of other housing services were disproportionately female. Approximately 67 per cent of people who had lived in social or assisted-living housing or had used housing services were women, while the percentage for non-users was only 60 per cent (table 6.10). The predominance of female residents was consistent with recent housing policies that gave priority to the placement in social housing of women with children who were fleeing domestic violence (Turner 2008; Special Priority Policy Research Taskforce 2011). Women also have lower incomes, on average, than do men, so female-headed households are more likely to qualify for social housing. Reflecting the relatively large supply of housing for seniors, seniors were slightly more likely to live in subsidized housing or use other housing services. Seniors comprised 18 per cent of users and 15 per cent of non-users. Immigrants were under-represented among residents of subsidized housing or users of housing services. While 77 per cent of those who had not lived in social, assisted-living, or independent-living housing or used housing services were immigrants, only 57 per cent of users were immigrants.

Recent immigrants were more likely than earlier immigrants to have lived in social housing or used other housing services: 51 per cent of users were recent immigrants, compared with only 44 per cent of non-users (table 6.10). Although users and non-users were equally likely to speak a non-official language at home, the plurality of recent immigrants among users was evident in their ethnic and racial backgrounds. Users were more likely than non-users to belong to racial minorities.

---

3 The small number of responses makes it impossible to comment on the use of individual services such as the Housing Help Centre in York Region.

Table 6.10   Social characteristics of non-users and users
of housing services

	Non-user (N = 1,470)		User (N = 76)	
	%	n	%	n
Woman	60	875	67	51
Senior	15	221	18	14
Immigrant	77	1,132	75	57
Recent immigrant	44	511	51	29
Non-official home language	61	888	57	43
Ethnicity:				
Canadian or British	8	121	8	6
Other European	21	311	14	11
Other minority	71	1,038	78	59
Household type:				
Couple	17	250	18	14
Other type	82	1,201	82	62
Childcare:				
Receive childcare	8	118	13	10
Need childcare	24	343	24	18
Household income:				
< $30,000	13	193	37	28
$30,00–$49,999	9	127	11	8
> $49,999	34	494	26	20

Source: Authors' Survey 2008

Satisfaction with Housing

Satisfaction with social housing, assisted-living housing, and other housing services was polarized between a majority who were satisfied with the services that they had received and a very dissatisfied minority. Of the seventy-six people who had lived in social or assisted-living housing or used one or more housing services, 73.9 per cent reported that they were somewhat or very satisfied. Of the remaining 22.8 per cent who were dissatisfied, more than half, 14.1 per cent, were very dissatisfied. Since the number of people living in social or assisted-living housing and using housing services was small, it is difficult to identify the types of housing or services that were considered unsatisfactory and those that were considered satisfactory. However, the shortages of social and assisted-living housing and other housing services in York Region are acute. More than five thousand households are on the waiting list for social housing, few locations offer housing information, and the region has fewer than 125 shelter beds (York Region 2007). In light of these shortages, the dissatisfaction was less prevalent than we had expected.

Summary and Conclusions

The main housing issue in York Region, as in all of Canada, is housing affordability. In York Region, low-income households and recent immigrants were more likely than were seniors to be living in housing that they could not afford. In both cases, low incomes were the cause of affordability problems. For many recent immigrants a combination of higher-than-average housing costs and below-average household incomes contributed to widespread affordability problems. Only a small percentage of seniors were experiencing affordability problems.

Affordability is an issue for both homeowners and renters. Unlike in the City of Toronto, where the majority of low-income households and recent immigrants are renters, in York Region homeownership is the dominant tenure. Although the majority of each vulnerable population lives in owned dwellings in York Region, homeownership does not always represent success in the housing market. High rates of ownership may be caused by the paucity of rental accommodation in the region and historically low interest rates for mortgages. Other research (Preston et al. 2009) has indicated that recent immigrants who want to live in York Region purchase housing because they cannot find suitable and affordable rental vacancies.

The supply of rental housing in York Region is insufficient to meet the needs of the growing low-income population and the increasing number of recent immigrants. With more than 80 per cent of the low-income population and almost 50 per cent of recent immigrants spending more than 30 per cent of total before-tax income on rent or ownership payments, additional affordable housing is needed. There is an emerging consensus that a national initiative is required to enlarge the supply of affordable housing by strategies such as the expansion of social housing and judicious housing subsidies (Federation of Canadian Municipalities 2008). Currently, in Ontario, rental units are created mainly through the development of condominium apartments that are purchased and rented out by investors. These additional rental units are often expensive. To promote the development of affordable rental units in York Region where housing prices are already high, the policies that have encouraged expansion of the supply of private rental units in cities outside Ontario should be reviewed, and those that are appropriate should be implemented.

The analysis here identifies concentrations of people in the midst of affluence who are experiencing housing-affordability problems in the southern part of the region. People with low incomes and recent immigrants who are spending more than 30 per cent or more than 50 per cent of total before-tax income on housing are more likely to live in southern York Region. In contrast, seniors who experience housing-affordability problems are dispersed throughout the region.

There was a mismatch between the provision of social housing and other housing services and the spatial distributions of recent immigrants and low-income households. Social housing and other housing services are concentrated in Newmarket and Richmond Hill, with very few being in the outlying areas that are labelled as the rest of York Region. Vaughan and the rest of York Region have a smaller percentage of social and assisted-living housing than their shares of the vulnerable populations. Markham and Aurora are better supplied with housing relative to the size of the recent immigrant and low-income populations, but the housing is still not sufficient, given the large vulnerable populations in these two municipalities. In Newmarket and Richmond Hill the supply of social and assisted-living housing relative to the senior and low-income populations is better than in any other part of the region.

The regional government should continue its efforts to expand the social housing stock throughout the region, paying particular attention to the supply of affordable housing in the south where the low-income population is underserved at the moment. This strategy will require working with residents who fear that the proximity of affordable housing threatens their property values. However, only by providing affordable housing where low-income households currently live can these households maintain the social contacts that are crucial for improving their economic situations (Chapple 2006).

The shortage of affordable housing in York Region is another illustration of the failure of neoliberalism. The supply of social housing is very limited relative to the growing numbers of low-income households and recent immigrants living in the region. Eligible individuals wait years for affordable housing units that not only offer a solution to their financial problems but, in the main, enhance access to other social infrastructure. Expansion of social housing near major arteries across the region, particularly in the south, would go a long way to addressing effectively the growing inequality and exclusion in the region.

7 Settlement Services in York Region

Introduction

In the past, recent immigrants usually settled in an inner-city neighbourhood for an extended time before accumulating enough capital to move to the suburbs (Murdie and Teixeira 2003). As a result most settlement services were located in the inner city. Settlement patterns have changed in the last couple of decades, and many new immigrants now settle in the suburbs as soon as they arrive (Murdie 2008). According to the census, 109,270 immigrants settled in York Region from 1996 to 2006.

As mentioned earlier, recent immigrants in this study refer to those who landed in Canada between 1996 and mid-May 2006, the time of the 2006 census. This definition was chosen because many studies have shown that, with significant changes in the composition of Canada's immigrant population in the last two to three decades, the settlement process has become much longer than it once was (for example see Borjas and Hilton 1996; Devoretz 1995).

Settlement is about acclimatizing to Canadian values and customs and to the Canadian way of living and doing things. Settlement is about fully integrating oneself into Canadian society, learning to speak its official languages, and sharing the rights and responsibilities of other Canadians, including being exposed to the same education, employment, housing, recreational, and other opportunities as are the Canadian born. The length and the outcome of this process depend on the characteristics and the drive of the immigrants. They are also conditional upon the social infrastructure that is available to enhance the process.

Like previous chapters, this chapter examines both sides of the settlement process by assessing recent immigrants' demand for settlement services and then analysing access to these services against their supply in York Region. It also examines immigrants' awareness of, use of, and satisfaction with these services.

Assessment of Demand

Accurate assessment of demand for settlement services is a difficult task. Depending on the composition of the recent-immigrant population in a given region, demand for settlement services may vary by number of agencies and types of services. The demographic and social attributes of the 109,270 recent immigrants who resided in York Region in May 2006 suggest diverse needs for all types of settlement services.

The majority of recent immigrants (57 per cent) were twenty-five to fifty-four years of age, prime years for active participation in the labour force. This is 12 per cent higher than the proportion of people from the same age cohort in the total population of York Region. They were also well educated: 40 per cent of immigrants who are fifteen years of age and older have a university education (that is, they hold a certificate, diploma, or degree), compared with only 26 per cent for the total population. It is unclear, though, how much of this education was obtained in Canada, where the recognition of foreign education credentials is a challenge for many Canadian employers. Not surprisingly, the unemployment rate in 2006 was 2 per cent higher for recent immigrants than for the total population in York Region (7.5 per cent versus 5.4 per cent).

With regard to place of birth, 72 per cent of the recent immigrants came from just ten countries (table 3.3). Notably, seven of them were Asian: China, Iran, India, South Korea, Sri Lanka, Pakistan, and Philippines. The other three were Eastern European: Russia, Ukraine, and Romania. None of these countries was among the traditional source countries for immigrants to Canada. Although the majority of recent immigrants speak English or French, Canada's official languages are often second languages for newcomers.

High unemployment rates, combined with large numbers of immigrants from Asian and other countries of birth outside Western Europe, suggest that many recent immigrants in York Region could benefit from job search and other employment services as well as orientation programs such as the Immigrant Settlement and Adaptation Program

(ISAP) and HOST. According to the 2006 census, 84 per cent of recent immigrants reported knowledge of English, and 11 per cent spoke neither English nor French (table 3.4); however, immigrants often overstate their fluency, and many are not able to meet the communications requirements that are demanded for many jobs. As a result, newcomers may have a high demand for language training.

Recent immigrants were heavily concentrated in the southern part of York Region (figure 3.3). Specifically, 92 per cent of them lived in the three municipalities of Markham, Richmond Hill, and Vaughan in 2006 (table 7.1). Lately, immigrants have begun to move northward to Aurora and Newmarket. In all parts of the region where recent immigrants are concentrating, high demand for settlement services is expected. Certainly, the agencies in the southern part of the region have the largest clienteles living nearby (table 7.1).

To analyse access to settlement services, for two reasons the focus is on those recent immigrants who are twenty-five years of age and older. First, younger immigrants are likely to attend schools, colleges, and universities in Canada, and therefore they are less likely than older adults to use settlement services. Second, the available census data did not allow us to separate adults who are most likely to be full-time students (those who are fifteen to twenty-two years of age) from those who are between twenty-three and twenty-four years of age.

Analysis of Supply

The supply of settlement services in a given region is typically assessed by three indicators: the number of service agencies, their capacity (including facility size, number of staff members, ratio of users to number of agencies or to number of staff members, and level of funding), and their accessibility to users. Accessibility, referring to how easy it is for immigrants to reach and obtain services from service providers, is affected by several factors, including physical distance, travel cost, capacity, and cultural sensitivity. For settlement services in Canada, user fees are not an issue, because most programs are provided free (or there is a nominal fee, such as a materials fee in ESL). The data compiled for this study indicate a list of settlement-service providers by location and types of service being offered, but there was no information about capacity. The accessibility analysis, therefore, focused on travel distance alone.

Three types of settlement services were examined here: English as a Second Language (ESL), Language Instruction for Newcomers (LINC),

Table 7.1 Distribution of recent immigrants and settlement service providers in York Region, 2006

| | Recent immigrants | | Settlement services | |
	Number	% of all immigrants	Number of agencies	Number of recent immigrants aged 25+ per agency
Aurora	3,065	2.8	1	2,040
Markham	45,775	41.9	5	6,454
Newmarket	3,835	3.5	1	2,555
Richmond Hill	29,125	26.7	5	3,991
Vaughan	25,480	23.3	9	1,996
Rest of York Region	1,915	1.8	0	1,340
York Region	109,195	100.0	21	3,618

Sources: Statistics Canada 2008; CIVC 2006

and general services (Immigrant Settlement and Adaptation Program). Different types of services are used with different frequencies. For example, immigrants enrolled in ESL or LINC programs attend classes daily or weekly; they are, therefore, distance sensitive. The users of ISAP visit service providers much less frequently, so they are less sensitive to travel distance.

Our discussion of accessibility focuses on the number and percentage of recent immigrants who live within three types of services areas: a 1.5 kilometre walk (assuming a walking speed of four kilometres per hour); a thirty-minute bus ride (or a fifteen kilometre distance, assuming travel speed of thirty kilometres per hour);[1] and a thirty-minute drive by automobile (or a twenty-five kilometre distance, assuming travel speed of fifty kilometres per hour). Analyses drew on catchment areas defined using geographic information systems.

1 Public transit in the suburbs (including York Region) has a lower frequency than in the City of Toronto. It could take longer than thirty minutes to travel fifteen kilometres if waiting time during non-rush hours is added.

English as a Second Language

Classes in English as a Second Language (ESL) are provincially funded programs that are open to everyone who needs to improve his or her English skills. At the time of the study they were found at sixty-two locations in York Region (see table 7.2 and figure 7.1) that together offered 158 classes. The majority of the classes were offered in Markham (65 per cent), Richmond Hill (20 per cent), and Vaughan (12 per cent), where recent immigrants were concentrated. On average, each class had a capacity of twenty-five seats, so the 158 classes could simultaneously accommodate 3,847 students (that is, the total number of seats). According to York Region Human Services Planning Coalition (2007, 19), some courses were offered more than once in a twelve-month period (that is, in cycles), and about 50 per cent of the students enrolled in more than one cycle.

There was no information on how many times the different courses were repeated, so it is not possible to calculate the ratio of annual enrolment (which refers to the total number of students enrolled in all classes) to the total spaces (that is, the product of the total number of seats and the number of cycles). The participation in ESL programs was low: only 15 per cent of recent immigrants who were twenty-five years and older (11,085 people out of 76,000) were taking ESL classes. If 50 per cent of the enrolments were repeaters, then only 8 per cent of the recent immigrants who were twenty-five years and older were taking ESL classes. It is not clear why participation in ESL was so low. If the ratio of recent immigrants to seats is calculated, it would range from 13:1 in Markham to 66:1 in Aurora, with an average of 20:1 for the entire region (see table 7.2); each service provider (with an average of sixty-two seats) serves 1,225 recent immigrants, assuming all recent immigrants need language training. Even if all the classes are repeated five times a year (which would mean shortening the courses to two-month cycles), there would still be a deficit in seats relative to the number of eligible recent immigrants (or those twenty-five years and older as earlier defined). This suggests strongly that the capacity of ESL programs in York Region is low.

In terms of accessibility, table 7.3 indicates that, in 2006, 40 per cent of the recent immigrants in the region lived within a 1.5 kilometre walking distance from an ESL agency; 94 per cent lived within a thirty-minute bus ride from an agency; and almost all lived within a thirty-minute drive from an agency.

Figure 7.1 Distribution of ESL programs in York Region, 2005

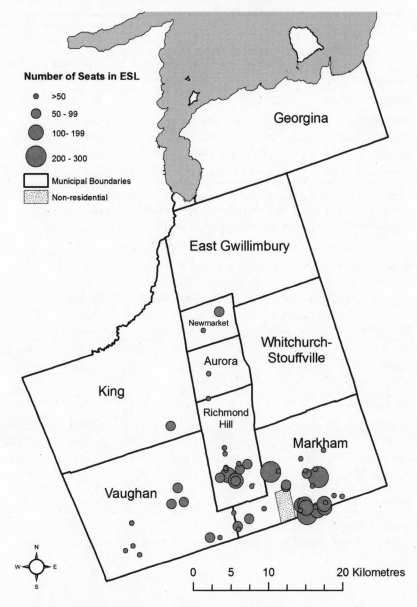

Source: York Region Human Service Planning Coalition 2007

Table 7.2   Distribution of ESL programs in York Region, 2005

Municipality	Number of locations	Number of classes	Number of seats	Ratio of recent immigrants (aged 25+) to enrolment*	Ratio of recent im- migrants (aged 25+) to seatsif classes are offered once per year
Aurora	1	1	37	174:1	66:1
Markham	30	102	2,460	9:1	13:1
Newmarket	4	5	125	24:1	20:1
Richmond Hill	14	31	750	14:1	27:1
Vaughan	13	19	475	38:1	38:1
York Region	62	158	3,847	14:1	20:1

* *Enrolment* refers to the total number of students enrolled in all cycles of ESL classes; there was no information on the number of cycles in which classes were offered.
Source: York Region Human Services Planning Coalition 2007

Table 7.3   ESL accessibility in York Region, 2006

Municipality	1.5 km walk		30 min. bus ride		30 min. drive	
	Recent immigrants*	%	Recent immigrants*	%	Recent immigrants*	%
Aurora	254	13.3	1,639	85.8	1,910	100.0
Markham	15,263	52.7	27,532	95.1	28,960	100.0
Newmarket	384	16.1	2,245	93.7	2,395	100.0
Richmond Hill	7,161	39.6	17,330	· 95.7	18,105	100.0
Vaughan	4,230	25.7	15,719	95.7	16,435	100.0
Others	4	0.4	204	18.8	812	74.8
York Region	27,297	39.6	64,669	93.9	68,617	99.6
Average catchment per agency or per 62 seats	479		1,135		1,204	

* Recent immigrants 25 years and older.
Source: Statistics Canada 2008; York Region Human Services Planning Coalition 2007

Language Instruction for Newcomers

Language Instruction for Newcomers (LINC) is a federally funded program, open to immigrants who are not yet Canadian citizens. Since most immigrants become Canadian citizens in three to five years, the analysis includes only recent immigrants who were twenty-five years and older and had been in the country for five years or less at the time of the 2006 census.

According to Citizenship and Immigration Canada–Ontario Region, LINC programs were offered at twelve facilities in York Region: four in each of Markham, Richmond Hill, and Vaughan (see table 7.4 and figure 7.2). No LINC classes were offered in any other municipalities. In total, these twelve programs offered forty-seven classes, with 835 seats, but the majority of the classes (57 per cent) and seats (52 per cent) were provided in Vaughan. On average, each class had eighteen seats, meaning that the LINC classes were smaller than the ESL classes. Each service provider, with an average of seventy seats, served 2,682 recent immigrants in York Region. If classes were offered in one cycle per year, the ratio of recent immigrants to seats ranged from 18:1 in Vaughan to 70:1 in Richmond Hill, with an average of 39:1 for the entire region (see table 7.4). Even if all the classes were repeated five times a year, there would still be a deficit in seats relative to the number of recent immigrants. This suggests that the capacity of LINC programs is much lower than that of ESL programs. Three of the twelve LINC program locations provided enhanced language training (ELT), one each in Markham, Richmond Hill, and Vaughan, and two of these were at locations where other LINC programs were also provided. Unlike the other LINC programs that provide basic language training for newcomers in English and French, ELT provides language training to help newcomers communicate in a work-related setting.

Owing to the small number of agencies and locations offering LINC, accessibility to LINC programs was much lower than that for ESL. On average, only 10 per cent of eligible recent immigrants lived within a 1.5 kilometre walking distance of a program. However, access by bus and automobile seemed to be fairly good, with 88 per cent of the eligible immigrants living within a thirty-minute bus ride, and 99 per cent within a thirty-minute drive, of these programs (see table 7.5).

Table 7.4   Distribution of LINC programs in York Region

Municipality	Locations	Classes	Seats	Ratio of recent immigrants* to seats if classes are offered once per year	Ratio of recent immigrants* to seats if classes are repeated five times per year
Markham	4	14	280	47:1	9:1
Richmond Hill	4	6	120	70:1	14:1
Vaughan	4	27	435	18:1	4:1
York Region	12	47	835	39:1	8:1

* Those who were 25 and older and had been in the country for five years or less at the time of the 2006 census.

Source: York Region Human Services Planning Coalition 2007; CIC-Ontario Region 2009

Table 7.5   LINC accessibility in York Region, 2009

Municipality	1.5 km walk Recent immigrants*	%	30 min. bus ride Recent immigrants*	%	30 min. drive Recent immigrants*	%
Markham	909	7.5	11,523	94.9	12,163	100.0
Richmond Hill	1,330	17.5	7,277	95.7	7,604	100.0
Vaughan	607	8.8	6,581	95.3	6,902	100.0
York Region	2,847	9.8	25,638	88.6	28,574	98.8
Average catchment per agency or per 70 seats	237		2,136		2,381	

* Those who were 25 and older and had been in the country for five years or less at the time of the 2006 census.

Source: York Region Human Services Planning Coalition 2007; CIC-Ontario Region 2009; Statistics Canada 2008

General Services

General services include welcome or orientation centres and agencies that provide housing and education information. Some are funded by the federal government (Citizenship and Immigration Canada, CIC) under the Immigrant Settlement Adaptation Program (ISAP). York

Figure 7.2 Distribution of LINC and ELT programs in York Region, 2009

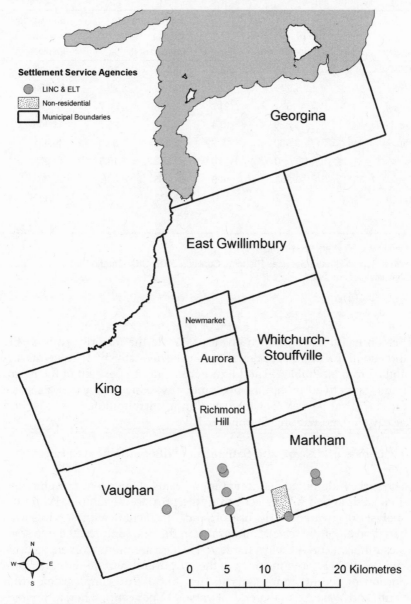

Source: CIC-Ontario Region 2009

Table 7.6   Distribution of general service agencies and accessibility in York Region, 2006

Municipality	Agencies	1.5 km walk		30 min. bus ride		30 min. drive	
		Recent immigrants*	%	Recent immigrants*	%	Recent immigrants*	%
Aurora	2	355	18.6	1,639	85.8	1,910	100.0
Markham	10	3,520	12.2	27,525	95.1	28,960	100.0
Newmarket	2	521	21.7	2,245	93.7	2,395	100.0
Richmond Hill	6	3,326	18.4	17,329	95.7	18,105	100.0
Vaughan	11	2,580	15.7	15,695	95.5	16,435	100.0
Others	1	0	< 1.0	202	18.6	975	89.9
York Region	32	10,303	14.9	64,635	93.8	68,780	99.8
Average catchment per agency		322		2,020		2,149	

*Those who were 25 years of age and above.

Source: York Region Human Services Planning Coalition 2007; CIC–Ontario Region 2009; Statistics Canada 2008

Region has thirty-two such agencies. While the majority were in the three southern municipalities, some had been established in Newmarket and Aurora (see table 7.6 and figure 7.3). Only 15 per cent of the recent immigrants lived within a 1.5 kilometre walking distance of a service provider, but 94 per cent lived within a thirty-minute bus ride, and nearly all lived within a 30-minute drive.

Awareness of, Use of, and Satisfaction with Settlement Services

The survey identified 540 recent immigrants, 43 per cent from the random sample and 57 per cent from the purposeful sample. While the analysis of awareness of, use of, and satisfaction with services was based on all of the recent immigrants in the two samples, the two samples differ in certain ways (table 7.7). There are more women, seniors, and people with low incomes in the purposeful sample. A higher proportion of recent immigrants in the purposeful sample came from South and West Asia (49 per cent versus 17 per cent), whereas the random sample contains more people from East Asia (61 per cent versus

Figure 7.3 Distribution of general service agencies in York Region, 2009

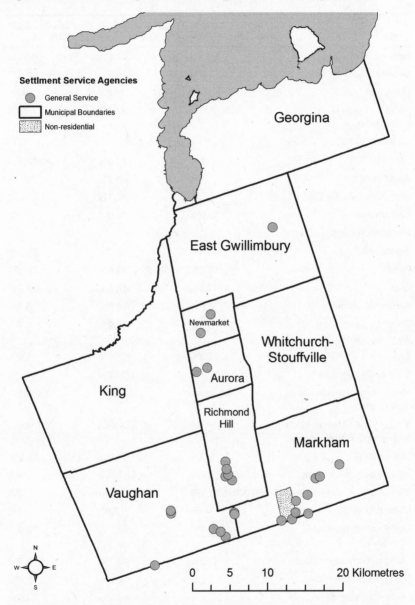

Source: York Region Human Services Planning Coalition 2007, CIC-Ontario Region 2009

Table 7.7 Profile of recent immigrants in the survey sample

	Random sample (N = 231)	Purposeful sample (N = 309)	Combined sample (N = 540)
Female	56.3%	69.9%	64.1%
Seniors	2.6%	14.6%	9.4%
Mean age	40	45.9	43.3
Mean age (age range) at immigration	31.6 (7–77)	42.4 (16–75)	37.8
Region of birth:			
East Asia	60.6%	28.8%	42.4%
South Asia	7.4%	30.1%	20.4%
West Asia / Middle East	10.0%	19.4%	15.4%
Eastern Europe	13.9%	12.6%	13.1%
Immigration class:			
Independent	33.8%	13.6%	22.2%
Family	18.6%	49.5%	36.3%
Business	7.8%	16.5%	12.8%
Refugee/claimant	2.6%	8.0%	5.7%
Temporary work visa / live-in caregiver	0.4%	0.9%	0.7%
BA+	55.3%	52.9%	53.9%
Educated in Canada	52.4%	21.7%	34.8%
Mean years of residence in York Region	4.5 years	2.2 years	3.1 years
Median time between landing and moving to York Region	3 years	0.75 years	1.7 years
Low income*	8.7%	36.6%	24.6%
Median personal income*	$20,000–$29,999	< $20,000	N/A
Median household income*	$60,000–$69,999	< $20,000	N/A
Mean household size	2.85	2.90	3.0
Using any employment services	23.4%	22.7%	23.0%
Using settlement services	17.3%	42.7%	31.7%
Using housing services	3.9%	6.5%	5.4%
Using education services	57.0%	48.1%	51.9%

Table 7.7   Profile of recent immigrants in the survey sample (*cont.*)

	Random sample (*N* = 231)	Purposeful sample (*N* = 309)	Combined sample (*N* = 540)
Using seniors services	0.0%	6.1%	3.5%
Mean types of services (5) used	1.02	1.26	1.1

* Note that 22% in the random sample and 29% in the purposeful sample did not report personal income, and 28% in the random sample and 47% in the purposeful sample did not report household income.

Source: Authors' Survey 2008

29 per cent); the proportions from Eastern Europe are similar (14 per cent versus 13 per cent). Moreover, a third of the recent immigrants in the random sample came as skilled immigrants, and half of those in the purposeful sample came as family-class immigrants; the proportion of business-class immigrants and the proportions of refugees and refugee claimants in the purposeful sample are double those in the random sample.

These differences explain why recent immigrants in the purposeful sample were, on average, ten years older than those in the random sample (forty-two years of age versus thirty-two years of age) when they landed in Canada. While the proportions holding a bachelor degree or higher are similar in both samples, the percentage having received Canadian education is much higher in the random sample than in the purposeful sample (52 per cent versus 22 per cent). Recent immigrants in the purposeful sample were more likely to settle directly in York Region upon landing. Table 7.7 reveals that, on average, recent immigrants from the random group moved to York Region three years after landing, compared with one year for those in the purposeful group.

The degree of vulnerability among recent immigrants varied. For the recent immigrant sample as a whole, 51 (9.4 per cent) were seniors, and 133 (24.6 per cent) lived in low-income households. Overall, 36.3 per cent had come as family-class immigrants, 22.2 per cent as independents, 12.8 per cent as business immigrants, and 5.7 per cent as refugees. Those who were more likely to report low income were the immigrants who were admitted under the business class or as refugees, who came from West Asia and the Middle East, who were older on arrival, who did not speak English at all at home, and who were newer to

York Region.The distribution patterns of sampled recent immigrants and low-income recent immigrants are similar to those of the entire recent-immigrant and low-income recent-immigrant populations in York Region (see figures 3.3 and 3.4).

Of the 540 recent immigrants, 32 per cent had used settlement services (table 7.7), with a higher proportion in the purposeful sample than in the random sample having used settlement services (43 per cent versus 17 per cent). Users of settlement services represented 60 per cent of the purposeful sample, and 35 per cent of the random sample. Few respondents had used two or more types of services.

Table 7.8 tabulates the variations among subgroups of recent immigrants and compares them with the total study participants with regard to use of settlement services. Whereas less than a third of recent immigrants used these services, almost half of low-income recent immigrants used them, and only 14 per cent of recent immigrants who were sixty-five years of age and older used them. As well, both the low-income and elderly recent immigrants were more likely to use settlement services than were their counterparts in the general population of the survey.

Awareness of Services

In the survey, awareness was measured by several questions that asked if the respondent had heard of specific immigrant service providers. These were some of the largest and most well-known human service providers in York Region, each with multiple locations, and they offer a variety of settlement services.

Table 7.9 shows that awareness of these immigrant service providers generally was low. Agency A did not provide settlement services. Agency B, present in many countries and providing a large variety of services to different age groups, was known by less than 40 per cent of the sampled recent immigrants. Agency C, which referred over three hundred names in the second stage of the sampling process, was recognized by less than 30 per cent of the respondents. Agency E, with an ethnic affiliation in its name, was known by less than 10 per cent of the respondents. Table 7.9 also shows that knowledge of these service providers varied between users and non-users of services, with higher levels of awareness (which, however, seldom surpassed 60 per cent) among users of social services.

Awareness decreased with income and increased with educational attainment. It was also closely tied to ethnicity. For example, 47 per cent

Table 7.8 Use of settlement services by subgroups of recent immigrants and total population

	Full sample	Using settlement services* (%)
Recent immigrants	540	31.9
Low income**	133	43.6
Seniors	51	13.7
Total participants	1,546	–
Low income**	214	27.1
Seniors	235	3.0

* Includes any services related to paid employment, self-employment, unemployment, and other employment-related matters.

** Drawing on Statistics Canada's low-income cut-offs, *low-income individuals* are defined as those living in single-person households with annual income below $20,000 or those living in multi-person households with annual household income below $30,000. All respondents so classified did not live alone; however, this number may not be representative of the whole sample, because only 870 respondents (56 per cent) answered the income questions.

Source: Authors' Survey 2008

of recent immigrants with European identity (particularly Jews from Russia and Eastern Europe) had heard of Agency E, compared with 7 per cent of those with other ethnic identities.

The importance of ethnicity was underscored by two other pieces of evidence from the survey data. First, over 80 per cent of respondents said that it was important to have agency workers who spoke their mother tongue (see table 7.10). Second, when asked how they had heard of each agency, they mentioned families and friends as the most important sources of information (see table 7.11). These results confirm the findings from the Longitudinal Survey of Immigrants to Canada, commonly known as LSIC (Schellenberg and Maheux 2007), as well as other research about the importance of ethnically based social networks and social capital in immigrant settlement and integration (Akbari and Harrington 2007; Akbari 2008; Deri 2005).

Use of Services

In the survey a series of questions was used to probe whether respondents used settlement services. The questions took the form of either "Have you ever used the settlement services provided by Y?" or "In the

Table 7.9 Awareness of selected settlement service agencies

Heard of	All recent Immigrants (*n* = 540)	Any human services		Settlement services	
		Users (*n* = 268)	Non-users (*n* = 272)	Users (*n* = 172)	Non-users (*n* = 368)
Agency B	39.1%	48.5%	38.6%	46.5%	42.1%
Agency C	26.9%	42.5%	35.7%	32.6%	42.1%
Agency D	15.9%	25.0%	16.2%	23.8%	19.0%
Agency E	8.7%	14.2%	7.7%	15.7%	8.7%

Source: Authors' Survey 2008

Table 7.10   Importance of agency workers speaking a client's mother tongue*

Importance	Respondents	%
Very important	94	65.7
Somewhat important	27	18.9
Not important at all	21	14.7
Don't know	1	0.7
Total	143	100.0

* The survey question was: "In deciding to use the services from an immigrant serving agency, how important was it for you that the workers at the agency/organization spoke your language?"
Source: Authors' Survey 2008

last five years, have you used the settlement services provided by Y?" In both, Y was the name of a service provider. The survey also contained a catch-all question: "Have you ever used any other settlement services in York Region?" A respondent who said yes to any service provider was deemed to be a user of settlement services.

Of the 540 recent immigrants in the survey, 172 (32 per cent) reported having used settlement services. Of these users, 161 (or 94 per cent) spoke a language other than English at home (see table 7.12). Although the social characteristics of users were similar to those of all recent immigrants in the region, users of settlement services differed from the non-users in several respects. Users were more likely to be recent immigrants born in Eastern Europe or East Asia than those born in South Asia or West Asia. While skilled and family-class immigrants were as

Table 7.11   Information sources for agencies

Information sources	Agency B (%)	Agency C (%)	Agency D (%)	Agency E (%)
Family	6.9	14.3	3.0	1.7
Friends	10.4	18.0	6.7	5.0
Neighbours	1.7	2.8	0.0	0.9
Agencies	3.3	8.3	5.4	0.4
Government officials, doctors, social workers, etc.	1.7	2.6	1.9	0.0
Places of worship	0.0	0.0	0.7	0.0
Newspapers	3.3	2.8	2.2	1.7
Internet	1.9	3.1	0.7	0.2
Television	0.7	0.4	0.4	0.2
Flyers	3.5	3.5	2.2	0.2
Welcome to Toronto Guidebook	0.6	1.1	0.4	0.4
Employers, co-workers	0.6	0.9	0.2	0.0
Other	7.0	3.0	3.0	1.5

Source: Authors' Survey 2008

Table 7.12   Settlement service users by home language, 2008

Home language	Respondents	%
Chinese, Cantonese, Mandarin	76	44.2
Russian, Ukrainian	32	18.6
Punjab, Tamil, Urdu, Hindi, Dari, Pashtu, other Indian	21	12.2
Farsi, Arabic, Farsi, Hebrew, other Middle Eastern	13	7.6
French, Italian, Spanish, other European	10	5.8
Korean, other Asian	9	5.2
English and one other language	9	5.2
English only	2	1.2
Total	172	100.0

Source: Authors' Survey 2008

likely to be users as non-users, business-class immigrants were more likely to be users than to be non-users (19 per cent versus 10 per cent). While the average age of both users and non-users was the same (between 36 and 37), there were more women (72 per cent versus 60 per cent) and university graduates (63 per cent versus 49 per cent) among the user group. Users of settlement services were more likely to have low incomes (34 per cent versus 20 per cent), and about 36 per cent of them had used other services as well. Among the non-users only 26 per cent had used other services.

During the survey ten settlement service agencies were mentioned to the respondents, who were asked to comment on their experiences with them (table 7.13). The survey revealed that, in general, usage of settlement services was low. The most frequently used agency was Agency C, since 70 per cent of the respondents had used its services. Next were the services provided by Agencies D and L, but only 20 per cent of the user respondents had used either of them. None of the other six agencies had been used by more than 7 per cent of the 172 respondents.

Reports on the usage of Agency C were high for two reasons. First, it has four locations in York Region. Second, as mentioned earlier, Agency C helped to recruit almost three hundred potential respondents in the second stage of the survey that produced the purposeful sample. Agency D also has four locations, yet its usage was much lower because fewer potential respondents came by way of Agency D.

Table 7.14 summarizes the usage patterns of three major settlement service providers. Four important observations can be highlighted. First, most of the users, ranging from 40 per cent to 47 per cent, reached the service locations by using public transit; another 27 per cent to 37 per cent visited the agencies by private automobile (either as driver or as passenger); and some (10 per cent to 23 per cent) walked.

Second, regardless of the different means of transportation, three-quarters of the surveyed users could reach the service in thirty minutes or less. This proportion is consistent with the calculations of travel time using the road network and transit routes. Respondents were mainly from the southern portion of York Region, where public transit is more readily available. Between 7 per cent and 21 per cent travelled for longer than thirty minutes but for less than one hour. Fewer than 10 per cent travelled for longer than one hour to get to the agency.

Third, the provision of settlement services within York Region is very important for the immigrants. The survey shows that only 8 per cent of

Table 7.13 Usage of the major settlement service providers in York Region

Settlement service providers (no. of locations)	Respondents*	Using services	Not using services**
Agency C (4)***	172	121	50
Agency D (4)	172	30	140
Agency E (1)	156	6	144
Agency H (3)	162	15	143
Agency I (1)	152	2	146
Agency J (1)	150	2	141
Agency K (1)	148	10	132
Agency L (1)	147	30	110

*   Including those who answered, "Don't know."
**   Excluding those who answered, "Don't know."
***   Agency C, founded to meet a shortage of services for immigrants in the post-war
       era, is today a multicultural agency that works with all immigrant communities
       having a shortage of established services. It provides educational, social, and
       employment services to help all immigrants in the Toronto area to attain self-
       sufficiency in Canadian society.
Source: Authors' Survey 2008

the 172 user respondents used services outside the region. The respondents apparently prefer using services located within the region.

Finally, only 8 per cent of the respondents said that, in the past ten years, they had not been able to get help when they needed it.

Satisfaction with Services

During the survey, respondents were asked to indicate on a four-point scale their degree of satisfaction with the service provided by each agency. In so far as any one person could have multiple responses to a particular service item, a multiple-response procedure was used to calculate a mean satisfaction score. The mean satisfaction scores – ranging between one and four, with one indicating "very satisfied," and four "very dissatisfied" – were related to selected socio-economic and demographic variables.

Overall, the mean satisfaction scores of 1.78 (table 7.15) indicated that recent immigrants who used settlement services were moderately

Table 7.14   Usage patterns of three major settlement service providers in York Region, 2008

	Agency C		Agency D		Agency L	
	No.	%	No.	%	No.	%
Have you used the settlement services provided?						
Yes	121	70.3	30	17.4	30	20.4
No	50	29.1	140	81.4	110	74.8
Don't know	1	0.6	2	1.2	7	4.8
Total	172	100.0	172	100.0	147	100.0
How did you usually get there?						
Other, varies, multiple	3	2.5	1	3.3	1	3.3
Walk	13	10.7	7	23.3	6	20.0
Public transit	57	47.1	14	46.6	12	40.0
Car (driver or passenger)	45	37.2	8	26.7	11	36.7
Don't know	3	2.5	0	0.0	0	0.0
Total	121	100.0	30	100.0	30	100.0
And how long does it usually take you to get there?						
0–30 minutes	90	74.4	25	83.3	23	76.7
31–60 minutes	26	21.5	4	13.3	2	6.7
> 60 minutes	2	1.7	1	3.3	3	10.0
Don't know	3	2.5	0	0.0	2	6.7
Total	121	100.0	30	100.0	30	100.0

Source: Authors' Survey 2008

satisfied with the services that they received. Although there are minor differences in satisfaction according to age and ethno-cultural background, the relationships are not statistically significant.

Summary and Conclusions

Suburban regional municipalities such as York Region are underserved by settlement service agencies (Sadiq 2004; Lim et al. 2005; Lo et al. 2007; Lo 2011). This study reveals that disparities also exist within

Table 7.15   Satisfaction with settlement services used

	Mean satisfaction score	N
Recent immigrants	1.78	259
Age at immigration:		
10–19	2.03	20
20–30	1.85	61
31–45	1.72	118
46+	1.73	58
Ethnicity:		
European	1.52	32
Indian, Asian, and other	1.82	226

Source: Authors' Survey 2008

the suburbs. In York Region the majority of recent immigrants resided in the southern urban municipalities. They have easier access to settlement services than do their counterparts who settled in the less urbanized part of the region in the north. Access to service, however, also varies among the urban municipalities in the region.

Ironically, Newmarket and Aurora, where the numbers of recent immigrants are low, provided relatively more services on a per capita basis than did Markham and Vaughan, which are home to the largest numbers of recent immigrants. This uneven pattern of accessibility has important implications for social inequality in the region and the provision of transit and social infrastructure.

The survey findings underscore the importance of providing settlement services within York Region. Only 8 per cent of respondents used services outside the region, and about 50 per cent of the users relied on public transit to reach settlement services. These findings have two implications. First, enhancing the public transit system is important in a region in which immigrants are moving to the less urbanized areas, where housing is more affordable, but public transit services are sparse and infrequent. Second, for many vulnerable recent immigrants the expenses incurred in using public transit to reach service agencies act as an access barrier. In this context, providing transportation subsidies to users of settlement services can improve service accessibility.

About one-third of the recent immigrants in the region were aware of and actually used settlement services. As they are more likely to be women, younger, better educated, and of European ethnicity, it raises the question of how well the information about settlement services targets "users" from other backgrounds (Lo et al. 2007). Extra efforts beyond the standard information or orientation package that is given to immigrants on arrival in Canada should be used to reach out to immigrants in a culturally sensitive way. Since use of services is tied to awareness of services, a crucial component of the settlement of immigrants is making newcomers aware that help with settlement needs is available. Many recent immigrants rely on their social networks to gain information about settlement. Perhaps funds should be allocated to helping recent immigrants develop bridging social capital that will expand their social networks and, thereby, result in more clients for settlement services.

Under the contemporary neoliberal regime, funding for settlement services has been a contentious issue. In the outer suburbs adequate and appropriate funding remains an ongoing challenge (Keung 2011a, 2011b). To address the funding disparities between central and outer suburban agencies, the latter should implement innovative service delivery models such as welcome centres and mobile services. Welcome centres that offer comprehensive service near public transit hubs improve access to services for recent immigrants. These welcome centres, where settlement agencies collaborate and coordinate their services, can also create cost savings for service providers. Although some clients have to travel farther to these hubs than to local agencies, overall the hubs minimize travel distance and travel time for users (Ismail and Smith 2013). A second model involves moving settlement workers to people in need instead of having recent immigrants travel to service locations. In addition to current programs that include settlement workers in libraries and schools, other models can include moving physical units such as motorized trucks and sending settlement workers to community events, and establishing non-moving structures such as portals on the Internet. These alternative models are especially useful in communities that have few services located nearby and where the immigrant population is small and dispersed.

Finally, the survey identifies unmet settlement need. Other than time and cost, program-eligibility requirements likely constrain the use of settlement services. As articulated by Citizenship and Immigration Canada, settlement policy primarily addresses the initial stage of settlement. In addition, CIC-funded settlement services are, for the most part, available to permanent residents and convention refugees only.

Immigrants are ineligible for settlement services after they have acquired Canadian citizenship. Women who may have childcare responsibilities during their early years in Canada, and men who take survival jobs immediately upon arrival, may have become ineligible for federally funded language programs when they are finally able to enrol in them. When settlement is viewed as a long-term process, it becomes clear that current settlement policies are inadequate or outdated. As the length of time required for immigrants to settle successfully has increased to well over a decade (Picot, Hou, and Coulombe 2008), policies need to recognize that immigrants' needs for settlement service often continue after they have become Canadian citizens. Only when the eligibility requirements for settlement services have been relaxed can those services contribute effectively to redressing the growing vulnerability of recent immigrants.

8 Conclusions

Observations

This study describes the geographies of vulnerability in a Canadian outer suburb, revealing poverty and other vulnerabilities in the midst of affluence and identifying shortages of social infrastructure that might redress multiple vulnerabilities. York Region, the subject of the case study, is a prime example of North American outer suburbs in which population growth and social diversification during the last two decades of neoliberal governance pose new planning challenges (Hanlon, Short, and Vicino 2009; Katz and Lang 2003; Kneebone and Berube 2013; Phelps and Wu 2011; Teaford 2008). Despite efforts to intensify land uses, to invest in transit, and to enhance social services, the number of vulnerable people has been growing faster than the social infrastructure. Pockets of vulnerability coexisting with affluence and high social status create complex geographies that call for innovative planning responses.

Our analysis underscores the significant presence of vulnerable populations in the outer suburbs, areas that are often considered to be affluent and prosperous. In 2006 the three vulnerable groups made up 30 per cent of York Region's population. These vulnerabilities were not mutually exclusive; nearly a fifth of the people in the vulnerable groups experienced more than one type of vulnerability (see table 3.1). The empirical analysis of York Region demonstrates that social exclusion is an important issue in outer suburbs even when aggregate statistics highlight their prosperity.

York Region's three vulnerable groups are distributed in different ways. The majority of recent immigrants live in the southern and urbanized part of the region where the transit network is the densest.

Low-income households are also found in large numbers in the southern part. However, their distribution is more dispersed than that of recent immigrants. There are pockets of people with low incomes in the northern half of the region. The spatial distribution of seniors is the mirror image of the other two distributions, with small percentages of seniors in the five large and urban municipalities and higher percentages in the rural parts of York Region. This study finds little correlation between social vulnerability and isolation from public transit in York Region, although a caveat is in order. Public transit in the region consists mainly of local bus service, which is linked along a few major arteries by express bus service. Although efforts are now underway to construct separate rights of way for the express buses, both systems currently struggle with traffic congestion and all of its associated problems. The varied geographies of vulnerability aggravate the challenge of ensuring equitable delivery of social services.

The degree of vulnerability varies among the three social groups. Seniors are better off than either recent immigrants or low-income people. With an average household income that is 81 per cent of the regional average, seniors are economically in a better position than recent immigrants, whose household income averages 70 per cent of that for the total population, and than the low-income population, which has an average household income equivalent to 23 per cent of the average in York Region. Of course, income is not a comprehensive measure of vulnerability. An affluent senior who does not drive (or no longer drives) may be isolated because public transportation is infrequent and because recreational and leisure services for this age group are in short supply at nearby community centres. The degree of vulnerability also varies among recent immigrants. Some with low income and limited language skills are in critical need of social services such as housing and employment services, while others only need information about educational and other social services.

Access to social services in York Region is marked by an urban-rural divide. Owing to the large and growing vulnerable populations in the southern part of the region, there is a geographical mismatch between the supply of and demand for the four services examined in this study. The underserved are concentrated in the two largest municipalities, Vaughan and Markham, where infrastructure development has not kept pace with population growth.

Access to the four social services also varies among the vulnerable populations across the region. Publicly funded elementary schools are the most widely available service, readily accessible in every part of the

region. In contrast, access to preschools and high schools is more limited for low-income households than for affluent residents. The supply
of social housing is uneven and insufficient to meet current needs, particularly where there has been an increase in the numbers of seniors
and low-income households. The same is true for settlement services,
which have not expanded as rapidly as has the population of recent
immigrants who are settling increasingly in the southern part of the
region. The employment services that are more readily available for
low-income people than for recent immigrants are concentrated along
Yonge Street, the major north-south artery, far from vulnerable populations in the eastern and western parts of the region. To address the
complex geographies of accessibility that do not fit with the popular
stereotypes of an affluent southern population and a marginalized
northern population requires sophisticated and thoughtful service
provision. Expansion of services would certainly address some of the
inequities uncovered by this study; however, wholesale expansion is
unlikely, and planners will have to take into account the varied geographies of vulnerability in a neoliberal environment of continuing scarci-
ty and fiscal restraint.

The survey specifically conducted for this study also speaks to the
relative importance of social services for vulnerable groups. As expected, residents of York Region use publicly funded education services the
most of all the services (table 8.1). Other social services are used less
often and mainly by specific segments of the population. In the survey
sample of 1,546 people, about 30 per cent used education, employment,
housing, settlement, and/or seniors services (table 8.1). This percentage is reduced to 15 per cent if the use of education services is excluded.
Although the percentage of the sample using services appears low, it
still indicates a fairly high rate of use. That approximately two-thirds of
the sample is representative of the entire population in the region suggests that the rate of use would have been higher if the sample had
consisted only of people from the three vulnerable groups.

The patterns of service use in this study raise questions about the
way in which providers of employment, housing, seniors, and settlement services can better serve their targeted clienteles. Social services
in general are more likely to be used by people with low incomes and
by recent immigrants than by seniors or the rest of the population.
Specifically, about half of the low-income and recent-immigrant populations used any service, compared with only one-third of seniors and
one-fifth of the rest of the population (table 8.1). Yet, of the four social

Table 8.1 Use of social services in York Region

	Full Sample		Education services (%)	Employment services (%)	Housing services (%)	Settlement services (%)	Seniors services (%)	Any services (%)	Any non-education services (%)
	N	%							
Total	1,546	100.0	64.1	16.7	4.9	11.1	4.3	30.9	15.1
Seniors	235	15.2	88.5	0.9	6.0	3.0	28.1	33.2	6.8
Low income*	214	13.8	51.4	25.2	12.1	27.1	8.9	54.7	33.2
Recent immigrants	540	34.9	48.0	23.0	5.4	31.9	3.5	49.6	48.0
Established immigrants**	640	41.4	75.8	12.8	4.2	NA	6.4	21.6	6.9
Canadian-born	336	21.7	64.0	13.7	5.7	NA	1.8	19.0	8.0

* Drawing on Statistics Canada's low-income cut-offs, *low income* is defined as individuals living in single-person households with annual income below $20,000, and individuals living in multi-person households with annual household income below $30,000. All respondents so classified do not live alone. However, this number may not be representative of the whole sample, since only 870 (56%) respondents answered the income questions.

** *N* = 640 including 17 who did not remember when they had immigrated to Canada.

Source: Authors' Survey 2008

services specifically studied, people with low incomes and recent immigrants are much less likely to use education services than are the other groups. After education services, employment services are the most used, yet the percentage of each vulnerable group using these services is low. Only about a quarter of low-income respondents and recent immigrants used employment services (table 8.1). Housing and seniors services are the least-used services. While the former can be explained by the limited supply of social housing in the region, it is unclear why so few seniors take advantage of the services intended explicitly for them. Finally, about one-third of the recent immigrants in the survey sample used settlement services. They are more likely to be women, young adults, well educated, and of European ethnicity. In light of the variable use of services, it is not surprising that the survey shows unmet demand for services. As an illustration, 35 per cent of recent immigrants requested more education services that may include English-language training, 14 per cent mentioned additional needs for employment services, 10 per cent wanted services for seniors, and 8 per cent indicated that they have unmet needs for settlement services.

The use of services is tied to awareness of services, yet awareness declines with income. As a result, some of the most vulnerable residents in York Region often have less access to services than do the more fortunate residents. These trends in awareness raise important questions for human service providers who struggle to make recent immigrants, people with low income, and seniors aware of the availability of services and other forms of help. Many in the vulnerable groups rely on their social networks for information and assistance. This raises another question: should resources be allocated to help vulnerable people develop social contacts with people outside their own social groups?

Despite their unmet needs, the vulnerable populations in York Region are moderately satisfied with the social services they have received. The overall satisfaction score with both employment and settlement services is slightly below two on a scale of one to four, in which one indicates a high level of satisfaction and four indicates a low level. Also, three-quarters of users of housing services are either very or somewhat satisfied with the services they have received. Residents of York Region who were born in Canada are more satisfied than are immigrants with the services they have received; for example, their satisfaction scores on employment services are respectively 1.73 and 2.08 (table 5.12). With regard to recent immigrants, half of the respondents reported more satisfaction with settlement services than with other services. There is the least satisfaction with employment services that have failed to address the labour market difficulties experienced by recent immigrants and people with low incomes. The dissatisfaction of recent immigrants in York Region and their high rates of low income indicate that current employment services are not meeting all the needs of recent immigrants.

The findings underscore the importance of public transit as a component of human service delivery. For the vulnerable groups in this study, public transit is an essential service. For example, 11 per cent of school-age children and youth and almost 50 per cent of recent immigrants travel to service locations on public transit. Only 75 per cent of recent immigrants can reach the services they use within thirty minutes, and about 10 per cent have to travel for more than an hour to service locations. The same is true for people with low incomes, who are more dispersed in York Region than are recent immigrants. If population growth in York Region continues into the less urbanized parts of the region, where public transportation infrastructure is sparse and the public transit system is least efficient, regional transit plans must ensure that people who do not have access to cars still have access to social services. Transport deficiency that makes people forgo opportunity leads to social exclusion (Church et al. 2000; Kenyon, Lyons, and Rafferty 2002).

By focusing on an outer suburb that has urbanized rapidly since 1971, this study has contributed to the growing literature about suburbs and about urban infrastructure. First, in the Canadian context, it complements the edited volume by Young, Wood, and Keil (2011), which focused on the "in-between" city, the amorphous area in North American cities that is neither central nor exurban. It also updates the works of Richard Harris (2004) who explored the history of Canadian suburbs, and Bunting et al. (2004) and Suttor (2007) who documented the distinct housing stock in Canadian outer suburbs. Second, the situation in York Region also illustrates the close links between networked physical infrastructure, such as transit and highway systems, and social infrastructure. In outer suburbs the access to social services is tied intimately to the availability of frequent and speedy public transit. Third, this case study points to a new suburban model that reconceptualizes contemporary suburbs in order to devise practical solutions for alleviating social inequities. The overarching goal is to avoid a repeat of the income polarization and social marginalization that has occurred in many post-war inner suburbs (Hulchanski 2010).

Moving Forward

As argued in the earlier chapters (chapter 1 in particular), little is known about the outer suburbs and the impacts of neoliberalism on their development. The York Region case study has illustrated some of the problems that may confront other rapidly growing and diversifying outer suburbs in North America. Contrary to popular images of suburbs as homogeneously white, middle-class, spacious, and clean, contemporary suburbs are susceptible to the social ills that are traditionally present in the centre and older parts of cities. Suburbs and cities are now adopting each other's previous path (Jackson 2006; Katz and Lang 2003). With economic globalization and the rise of a knowledge economy, many neighbourhoods in central cities are gentrifying, attracting young, affluent, economically active, and environmentally conscious people who have largely grown up in suburbs. Attracted by the convenience and apparent sustainability of "walkable" neighbourhoods with nearby amenities, house-hunters bid up prices and displace those who are less affluent and financially secure. Suburbs are increasingly home to recent immigrants, seniors, and low-income individuals, while their traditional form and structure – segregated land uses, low-density housing, and automobile dependency – remain. This study shows that newer outer suburbs may well follow the path of decline that is occurring in the older inner suburbs that sprang up in the post-war years in Toronto (Hulchanski 2010; Walks 2011) and elsewhere (Cisneros et al. 2009; Duany, Plater-Zyberk, and Speck 2001; Lucy and Phillips 2000). Unlike central cities and inner suburbs, outer suburbs that emerged largely during the neoliberal age lack social housing. As a result, vulnerability is often not readily apparent. The housing stock helps to maintain an upper-middle- or middle-class appearance. Suburbs are increasingly similar to city centres in their demographic composition and economic functions while they retain their traditional built form. They are marked by increasing diversity and social inequality (Alba et al. 1999; Marcelli 2004; Murdie and Teixeira 2003), but, as this study shows, much social vulnerability is found in small pockets that are dispersed across the suburban landscape and often hidden from public scrutiny. Coupled with the spatial spread of vulnerability, its invisibility creates challenges for the planning of social services that might redress social inequality. Without the legacy of social infrastructure in central neighbourhoods (Bunting et al. 2004; Clutterbuck and Howarth 2002), municipal governments in the outer suburbs are torn between the competing demands for the infrastructure that will reduce social vulnerability and the infrastructure that is needed to maintain development. In this context the spatial dispersal of vulnerability exacerbates the technical and political difficulties of providing social infrastructure that will reduce diverse vulnerabilities.

To suggest the ways in which the existing social services in outer suburbs can evolve to better meet the needs of vulnerable groups such as recent immigrants, low-income people, and seniors, this study adopts a social inclusion framework that views inclusion as both a goal and a process (Omidvar and Richmond 2003). It involves the removal of barriers to opportunities in the housing market, the labour market, education, and other social services, and the closing of gaps between those who are at risk of poverty and isolation and those who are not. A key finding from this study – that only a small proportion of people living in York Region are aware of and actually use existing settlement, housing, and employment services – lends support to Reitz's (1995) assertion that under-utilization of services can result from barriers to access. In this outer suburb, population growth has occurred without equivalent expansion of social infrastructure primarily as a result of neoliberal governance. Without the legacy of the social infrastructure developed in the 1960s and 1970s, the outer suburb, growing during a period of roll-out neoliberalism, has a shortage of social infrastructure, which may increase the size of its vulnerable populations and which certainly heightens inequality and the vulnerability of those who are already struggling with low incomes and the challenges of aging and settling in a new society.

A two-pronged strategy is needed to address the disadvantages suffered by the growing vulnerable populations in the region. By reducing barriers to the use of social services, it is expected that increasing awareness and use of services can improve the quality of life for seniors, recent immigrants, and people with low incomes. Enhancing the supplies of services will also improve access to services that have the potential to reduce social exclusion and the vulnerable populations in the region. The required investments in social infrastructure will only succeed if funding is flexible and sustained. Project-based funding associated with roll-out neoliberalism often reduces both the level and the quality of services (Omidvar and Richmond 2003).

Multiple and diverse barriers inhibit use of services. They range from inadequate volume of services to inaccessible services. As the analysis has shown, access extends well beyond geographical accessibility. For example, many people prefer to speak to service providers in their mother tongue. Wang, Rosenberg, and Lo (2008) found that Chinese immigrants in Toronto prefer to consult Chinese physicians because of the role that cultural nuances can play in communicating and understanding health issues. In a study of the utilization of services in New York City's social welfare system by female immigrants, Lutz (1994) found that the strongest predictor of the use of an agency's services was the number of persons of the same ethnicity employed by that agency. In a study of approximately thirteen thousand outpatients of the Los Angeles County Department of Health, researchers found positive effects of an ethnic match between patient and therapist on treatment outcomes for Mexican Americans (Sue et al. 1991). Wu and Windle (1980) also reported that the larger the staff proportion of a particular minority group in a mental health centre, the higher the utilization rate by that minority. The effect of ethnic matching between users and service providers is clear. In addition to improving utilization rates, ethnic matching can also reduce program costs (Snowden, Hu, and Jerrell 1995).

To ensure sufficient and responsive services for vulnerable individuals that will address their current needs and permanently reduce their vulnerability, multiple methods of service delivery should be considered. The traditional model of providing services in a fixed location with high population density may not work in suburbs such as York Region where mobility is constrained by the low-density and automobile-oriented landscape. Access to affordable and appropriate transportation is consistently listed as a major issue. The current transit system has improved considerably since the introduction of Viva bus service in September 2005. However, this surface transit service is viewed as less convenient and efficient than the subways and other forms of rapid transit that operate in their own rights of way. Viva service is also limited to major arteries, so it does not serve many of the rural and northern parts of York Region. When planning social services such as those studied here, planners must counteract the tendency of fixed rail systems to reinforce the concentration of transit services along existing routes. Public transit in the region is often too expensive for the three vulnerable populations. While it is understandable that providing public transit in low-density suburbs is expensive, in addition to furthering the transportation infrastructure in York Region, a socially inclusive approach should mitigate the expenses incurred when vulnerable individuals use public transit to reach human service providers.

The spatial analyses in this study indicate that social services in York Region are inequitably distributed, not only between rural and urban parts of the region but also within the region's urban municipalities. A key finding is that only a small proportion of those living in York Region are aware of existing settlement, housing, education, and/or employment services. Lack of knowledge about the availability of social services can make entering the labour market, securing affordable and adequate housing, and settling in a new region very challenging and stressful. Many immigrants who settle in York Region may be unaware of the availability of social services and their eligibility for these services. Low-income individuals may not have the resources needed to find information. To heighten awareness of services and increase usage, all social services should be publicized in as many different media as possible.

Service usage is likely promoted best by a community engagement approach that values local inputs and facilitates horizontal ties in a context in which the values of diverse groups are seen as equally important to society as a whole. Engaging vulnerable groups in decisions about social infrastructure provision offers the most equitable and effective strategies for addressing inequality (Sandercock 2003). At present, different levels of government fund different infrastructure needs, and intergovernmental collaboration is seen more often in hard infrastructure investment than in human service provision. The Canada-Ontario Immigration Agreement, signed in November 2005, was an exception. Through the agreement the federal government committed $920 million in new immigration funding over five years to help recent immigrants successfully integrate into Ontario communities and achieve their full potential. It included a provision to involve the City of Toronto and other Ontario municipalities, through the Association of Municipalities in Ontario, in the planning and discussion of immigration and settlement issues. This agreement, which has now expired, marks one of the few occasions that all three levels of government were acknowledged to have a role in planning the services for immigrants.

The merits of planning for human services at the local level are being explored currently through Local Immigration Partnerships, a collaborative framework designed to discuss local solutions for the successful integration of immigrants (Wayland 2011). The initiative brings together diverse stakeholders to propose strategies for addressing immigrants' needs regarding access to labour markets, the education system, housing, and community and neighbourhood services. In York Region the Local Immigration Partnership, which is chaired and organized by the regional government, includes representatives from settlement service providers, school boards, hospitals, the United Way of

York Region, and local governments. The Community Partnership Council that is central to the Local Immigration Partnership in York Region is an exciting experiment in community engagement that merits continued observation and evaluation. Although it is not yet clear whether it has contributed to reducing the growing vulnerability in the region, its activities may yet serve as a useful model for future efforts in planning and implementing social services in order to increase social justice in York Region. For the moment, the Local Immigration Partnerships remain solely advisory and planning bodies (Wayland 2011). In York Region there is an effort to move beyond this advisory role. The Community Partnership Council's report entitled *Leading Change for a Stronger Community: Community Partnership Council Collective Action Plan, 2012–2015 (Action Plan)* recommends 126 specific actions to promote successful immigrant settlement and has been adopted by the regional government.

Closing Reflections

This study has punctured the neoliberal imaginary of suburbs as wealthy and prosperous spaces. An outer suburb such as York Region is home to an increasing number of people at risk of specific vulnerabilities. It appears, as Peck (2011, 884) notes, that "the suburb failed even to secure a stable definitional identity on its quiet path to dominance." Social inequality in the outer suburbs is similar to that observed in central cities (Boudreau, Keil, and Young 2009; Hulchanski 2010; Walks 2011). The supply of social infrastructure in outer suburbs is simply insufficient to meet current needs. Following an era of roll-back neoliberalism, the availability of services has not grown at the same rate as have the vulnerable populations or even the total population. Underfunding has proved to be an ongoing problem for the growing suburban municipalities such as those in York Region (Pembina Institute 2007, 48).

The social and geographical variability in vulnerability revealed by the analysis compounds the challenges of underfunding. With limited resources, service providers are asked to adopt innovative practices to serve their clienteles, while struggling to maintain current levels of service. Roll-back neoliberalism has constrained not only the overall supply of services but also the capacity to respond effectively to diverse service needs at different locations within the outer suburbs. In this context the gaps between demand and supply of services are larger for low-income households and recent immigrants than for seniors. The heightened vulnerability of low-income households and recent immigrants does more than contradict popular images of the affluent outer suburbs; it also threatens their continued affluence. Without effective services, low-income households and recent immigrants will not make much social and economic progress, with potentially serious consequences for their own social inclusion and possibly that of their children (Murie and Musterd 2004).

The impacts of neoliberalism warrant attention (Hackworth 2008). The spatial analysis of the data on service demand and supply, combined with the survey information on awareness of, use of, and satisfaction with services, has established starkly that roll-back neoliberalism has affected the outer suburbs. Although service providers complain that a growing emphasis on short-term project funding and continual performance measurement limits their ability to meet the growing and diverse needs of vulnerable populations, this study has only touched on this aspect of roll-out neoliberalism. Interrogating the impacts of infrastructure retrenchment and alignment is thus a task for the future.

To reiterate, York Region is but one of the many suburbs on the edge of North America's metropolitan areas. The trends in York Region are not unique. In North American suburbs people are aging in place, immigration levels are rising, and income polarization is worsening. Shaped by larger globalization and neoliberalization processes, these trends have been documented separately in some recent publications such as Andrews and Phillips (2005) on aging, Kneebone and Berube (2013) and Sharma (2012) on poverty, and Teixeira, Li, and Kobayashi (2011) on immigration. This study underscores the ways in which the interaction of these trends, especially between immigration and income polarization, can create complex geographies of vulnerability in suburbs. Housing, transportation, employment, and the provision of education and other basic services in suburbs and city centres alike are essential to the long-term well-being and effective functioning of metropolitan areas. A wide range of public infrastructure or social services that are easily accessible to vulnerable populations ensures the existence of opportunities for them. In this regard, regions – suburbs or not – should be equipped with aid that cuts across jurisdictional lines.

References

Akbari, A.H. (2008). The role of networks in economic integration of new arrivals. *Our Diverse Cities, 5,* 88–90.

Akbari, A.H., & Harrington, J.S. (2007). *Initial location choice of new immigrants to Canada.* Atlantic Metropolis Centre Working Paper.

Alba, R.D., Logan, J.R., Stults, B.J., Marzan, G., & Zhang, W. (1999). Immigrant groups in the suburbs: A reexamination of suburbanization and spatial assimilation. *American Sociological Review, 64*(3), 446–60. http://dx.doi.org/10.2307/2657495

Alboim, N., Finnie, R., & Meng, R. (2005). The discounting of immigrants' skills in Canada: Evidence and policy recommendation. *IRPP Choices, 11*(2), 2–23.

Andrews, G.J., & Phillips, D.R. (2005). *Ageing and place: Perspectives, policy, and practice.* London, New York: Routledge.

Anisef, P., & Lanphier, M. (2003). Introduction: Immigration and accommodation of diversity. In P. Anisef & M. Lanphier (Eds.), *The world in a city* (pp. 3–18). Toronto: University of Toronto Press.

Apparicio, P., Cloutier, M.-S., & Shearmur, R. (2007). The case of Montreal's missing food deserts: Evaluation of accessibility to food supermarkets. *International Journal of Health Geographics, 6*(4), 13 pages.

Ballingall, A. (2013, 10 July). Toddler dies at unlicensed Vaughan day care now ordered shut. *Toronto Star.* Accessed 26 July 2013. http://www.thestar.com/news/gta.html.

Banister, D., & Bowling, A. (2004). Quality of life for the elderly: The transport dimension. *Transport Policy, 11*(2), 105–15. http://dx.doi.org/10.1016/S0967-070X(03)00052-0

Basu, R. (2002). Active and dormant spaces: A look at the geographical response to school based care. *Journal of Planning Education and Research, 21*(3), 274–85. http://dx.doi.org/10.1177/0739456X0202100305

Basu, R. (2004). The rationalization of neoliberalism in Ontario's public education system, 1995–2000. *Geoforum, 35*(5), 621–34. http://dx.doi.org/10.1016/j.geoforum.2004.03.003

Beck, U. (1993). *Risk society: Towards a new modernity.* London: Sage Publications.

Beiser, M. (1999). *Strangers at the Gate: The "boat people's" first ten years in Canada.* Toronto: University of Toronto Press.

Blackman, T., Brodhurst, S., & Convery, J. (Eds.). (2001). *Social care and social exclusion: A comparative study of older people's care in Europe.* New York: Palgrave. http://dx.doi.org/10.1057/9781403914071.

Blaikie, P., Cannon, T., Davis, I., & Wisner, B. (2005). *At risk: Natural hazards, people's vulnerability, and disasters* (2nd ed.). London: Routledge.

Blumenberg, E. (2008). Immigrants and transport barriers to employment: The case of Southeast Asian welfare recipients in California. *Transport Policy, 15*(1), 33–42. http://dx.doi.org/10.1016/j.tranpol.2007.10.008

Blumenberg, E., & Evans, A.E. (2007). Growing the immigrant transit market: Public transit use and California immigrants. Transportation Research Board 86th Annual Meeting Compendium of Papers. CD-ROM.

Borjas, G.J., & Hilton, L. (1996). Immigration and the welfare state. *Quarterly Journal of Economics, 111*(2), 575–604. http://dx.doi.org/10.2307/2946688

Boudreau, J.-A., Hamel, P., Jouve, B., & Keil, R. (2007). New state spaces in Canada: Metropolitanization in Montreal and Toronto compared. *Urban Geography, 28*(1), 30–53. http://dx.doi.org/10.2747/0272-3638.28.1.30

Boudreau, J.-A., Keil, R., & Young, D. (2009). *Changing Toronto: Governing urban neoliberalism.* Toronto: University of Toronto Press.

Bourne, L.S. (1996). Reinventing the suburbs: Old myths and new realities. *Progress in Planning, 46*(3), 163–84. http://dx.doi.org/10.1016/0305-9006(96)88868-4

Bourne, L.S., Bunce, M., Taylor, L., Luka, N., & Maurer, J. (2003). Contested ground: The dynamics of peri-urban growth in the Toronto Region. *Canadian Journal of Regional Science, XXVI*(2 & 3), 251–70.

Brenner, N., & Theodore, N. (Eds.). (2002). *Spaces of neoliberalism.* Oxford: Blackwell. http://dx.doi.org/10.1002/9781444397499.

Brodie, J. (2007). Reforming social justice in neoliberal times. *Studies in Social Justice, 2*(1), 93–107.

Bunting, T., Filion, P., & Walks, A.R. (2004). The uneven geography of housing affordability stress in Canadian metropolitan areas. *Housing Studies, 19*(3), 361–93. http://dx.doi.org/10.1080/0267303042000204287

Burchell, G., Gordon, C., & Miller, P. (1991). *The Foucault effect: Studies in governmentality.* Chicago: University of Chicago Press. http://dx.doi.org/10.7208/chicago/9780226028811.001.0001.

Byers, M., Kennedy, J., McBurney, M., & Robertson, H. (1976). *Rural roots: Pre-Confederation buildings of the York Region of Ontario*. Toronto: University of Toronto Press.

Cain, P. (2013, 19 March). Income by postal code: Mapping Canada's richest and poorest neighbourhoods. *Global News*. Accessed 26 May 2014. http://globalnews.ca/news/370804/income-by-postal-code/

Catholic Community Services of York Region. (2001). Embracing diversity report. One Day Symposium on Ethnicity, Access, and Participation. Richmond Hill, ON: Catholic Community Services of York Region.

CBC. (2012, 3 February). Immigrant families under pressure. http://www.cbc.ca/toronto/features/greatexpectations/2012/02/immigrant-families-under-pressure.html.

Chapple, K. (2006). Overcoming mismatch: Beyond dispersal, mobility, and development strategies. *Journal of the American Planning Association, 72*(3), 322–36.

Chiras, D., & Wann, D. (2003). *Superbia: 31 ways to create sustainable neighbourhoods*. Gabriola Island, BC: New Society Publishers.

Chui, T., Tran, K., & Maheux, H. (2007). *Immigration in Canada: A portrait of the foreign-born population, 2006 census*. Ottawa: Ministry of Industry.

Church, A., Frost, M., & Sullivan, K. (2000). Transport and social exclusion in London. *Transport Policy, 7*(3), 195–205. http://dx.doi.org/10.1016/S0967-070X(00)00024-X

Cisneros, H.G., Singer, A., Hardwick, S.W., & Brettell, C.B. (2009). *Twenty-first-century gateways: Immigrant incorporation in suburban America*. Washington, DC: Brookings Institution Press.

CIVC. (2006). Custom tabulations from Community Information and Volunteer Centre of York Region. December.

Clarke, P.J., Marshall, V.W., Ryff, C.D., & Rosenthal, C.J. (2000). Well-being in Canadian seniors: Findings from the Canadian Study of Health and Aging. *Canadian Journal on Aging/La Revue Canadienne du Vieillissement, 19*(02), 139–59. http://dx.doi.org/10.1017/S0714980800013982

Clutterbuck, P., & Howarth, R. (2002). *Toronto's quiet crisis: The case for social and community infrastructure investment*. Toronto: Centre for Urban and Community Studies.

Collin, J.P., & Poitras, C. (2002). La fabrication d'un espace suburbain : La Rive-Sud de Montréal. *Recherches Sociographiques, 43*, 275–310. http://dx.doi.org/10.7202/000539ar

Council of the Regional Municipality of York. (2009). *Official plan*. Newmarket, ON: York Region.

Cowen, D. (2005). Suburban citizenship: The rise of targeting and the eclipse of social rights in Toronto. *Social & Cultural Geography, 6*(3), 335–56. http://dx.doi.org/10.1080/14649360500111212

Cutter, S. (2003). The vulnerability of science and the science of vulnerability. *Annals of the Association of American Geographers, 93*(1), 1–12. http://dx.doi .org/10.1111/1467-8306.93101

The Daily. (2007, 22 June). Government spending on social services, 1989 to 2007. Ottawa: Statistics Canada.

Data Management Group. (2009). *Travel survey summaries for the Greater Toronto and Hamilton Area: Fifth report of the 2006 TTS series*. Toronto: University of Toronto. Accessed 9 May 2011. http://www.dmg.utoronto.ca/transportation-tomorrowsurvey/2006/travel_summaries_for_the_gtha.html#york.

DeBresson, C., & Barker, S. (1998). *Looking to the 21st century: Infrastructure investments for economic growth and for the welfare and well-being of Canadians*. Ottawa: Industry Canada.

Denton, F., and Spencer, B. (2001). *Immigrant newcomers to Ontario: The distribution of people and settlement funding*. Report commissioned by CIC-OASIS.

Deri, C. (2005). Social networks and health service utilization. *Journal of Health Economics, 24*(6), 1076–107. http://dx.doi.org/10.1016/j.jhealeco.2005.03.008

De Voretz, D.J. (1995). New issues, new evidence, and new immigration policies for the twenty-first century. In D.J. De Voretz (Ed.), *Diminishing returns: The economics of Canada's recent immigration policy* (pp. 1–30). Toronto, Vancouver: Howe Laurier Institute.

Duany, A., Plater-Zyberk, E., & Speck, J. (2001). *Suburban nation: The rise of sprawl and the decline of the American dream*. New York: North Point Press.

Engeland, J., & Lewis, R. (2005). *Evolving housing conditions in Canada's metropolitan areas, 1991–2001: Trends and conditions in census metropolitan areas*. Ottawa: Canada Mortgage and Housing Corporation.

England, K., & Ward, K. (Eds.). (2007). *Neoliberalization: States, networks, peoples*. Malden, MA: Blackwell. http://dx.doi.org/10.1002/9780470712801.

Esping-Andersen, G. (1990). *The three worlds of welfare capitalism*. Cambridge: Polity Press.

Federation of Canadian Municipalities. 2008. *Quality of life in Canadian communities: Trends & issues in affordable housing and homelessness*. Ottawa: Federation of Canadian Municipalities.

Fiedler, R., & Addie, J.P. 2008. *Canadian cities on the edge: Reassessing the Canadian suburb*. Occasional Paper Series, vol. 1, issue 1. Toronto: City Institute, York University.

Fotheringham, A.S., & Rogerson, P.A. (2008). *Handbook of spatial analysis*. London, UK, and Thousand Oaks, CA: Sage Publications.

Frenette, M., & Morissette, R. 2003. *Will they ever converge? Earnings of immigrants and Canadian-born workers over the last two decades*. Research Paper

Series, catalogue no. 11F0019MIE — No. 215. Ottawa: Statistics Canada, Analytical Studies Branch. http://dx.doi.org/10.2139/ssrn.473861.

Friedman, A. (2002). *Planning the new suburbia: Flexibility by design.* Vancouver: UBC Press.

Frisken, F. (2007). *The public metropolis: The political dynamics of urban expansion in the Toronto region, 1924–2003.* Toronto: Canadian Scholars Press.

Frisken, F., & Wallace, M. (2002). *The response of the municipal public service sector to the challenge of immigrant settlement.* Chapter 2, pp. 33–64. Toronto: Citizenship and Immigration Canada, Ontario Region, OASIS.

Funston, M. (2005, 16 May). Peel social services in crisis. *Toronto Star*, pp. B1, B4.

Ghosh, A., & Ingene, C. (1991). *Spatial analysis in marketing: Theory, methods, and applications.* Greenwich, CT: JAI Press.

Giddens, A. (1990). *The consequences of modernity.* Stanford, CA: Stanford University Press.

Gombu, P. (2010, 20 April). Municipal elections: 5 burning issues York region. It's all about growth, from servicing denser development to preserving green space. *Toronto Star*, p 2.

Gough, L., & Eisenschitz, A., with McCulloch, A. (2006). *Spaces of social exclusion.* New York: Routledge.

Graham, S. (2000). Constructing premium network spaces: Reflections on infrastructure networks and contemporary urban development. *International Journal of Urban and Regional Research, 24*(1), 183–200. http://dx.doi.org/10.1111/1468-2427.00242

Graham, S., & Marvin, S. (2001). *Splintering urbanism, networked infrastructure, technological mobilities and the urban condition.* London: Routledge. http://dx.doi.org/10.4324/9780203452202.

Gray, J. (2000). Inclusion: A radical critique. In P. Askonas & A. Stewart (Eds.), *Social inclusion: Possibilities and tensions* (pp. 19–36). New York: St Martin's Press.

Greater Toronto Transportation Authority. (2008). *The big move: Transforming transportation in the Greater Toronto and Hamilton Area.* Toronto: Metrolinx.

Grech, C. (2008, 25 January). Markham residents show up to fight 16th Avenue widening. *The Liberal*, p. 1.

Hackworth, J. (2008). The durability of roll-out neoliberalism under centre-left governance: The case of Ontario's social housing sector. *Studies in Political Economy, 81*, 7–26.

Hackworth, J., & Moriah, A. (2006). Neoliberalism, contingency and urban policy: The case of social housing in Ontario. *International Journal of Urban and Regional Research, 30*(3), 510–27. http://dx.doi.org/10.1111/j.1468-2427.2006.00675.x

Hanlon, B., Short, J.R., & Vicino, T.J. (2009). *Cities and suburbs: New metropolitan realities in the US*. New York: Routledge.

Harris, R. (2004). *Creeping conformity: How Canada became suburban, 1900–1960*. Toronto: University of Toronto Press.

Harris, R., & Larkham, P. (1999). *Changing suburbs: Foundation, form and function*. London: E and FN Spon.

Hayden, D. (2003). *Building suburbia: Green fields and urban growth, 1820–2000*. New York: Pantheon Books.

Heisz, A., & Schellenberg, G. (2004). Public transit use among immigrants. *Canadian Journal of Urban Research, 13*(1), 170–91.

Hiebert, D. (1999). Local geographies of labour market segmentation: Montreal, Toronto, and Vancouver, 1991. *Economic Geography, 75*(4), 339–69. http://dx.doi.org/10.2307/144476

Hiebert, D., Germain, A., Murdie, R., Preston, V., Renaud, J., Rose, D., . . ., & Murnaghan, A.M. (2006). *The housing situation and needs of recent immigrants in the Montréal, Toronto, and Vancouver CMAs: An overview*. Ottawa: Canada Mortgage and Housing Corporation.

Hiebert, D., & Mendez, P. (2008). *Settling in: Newcomers in the Canadian housing market, 2001–2005*. Working Paper Series no. 08–01. Vancouver: Metropolis British Columbia, Centre of Excellence for Research on Immigration and Diversity.

Hine, J., & Mitchell, F. (2001). Better for everyone? Travel experiences and transport exclusion. *Urban Studies (Edinburgh, Scotland), 38*(2), 319–32. http://dx.doi.org/10.1080/00420980020018619

Hou, F., & Picot, G. (2003). *Visible minority enclave neighbourhoods and labour market outcomes of immigrants*. Ottawa: Statistics Canada, Analytical Studies Branch.

Hulchanski, J.D. (2010). *The three cities within Toronto: Income polarization among Toronto's neighbourhoods, 1970–2005*. Toronto: Cities Centre, University of Toronto.

Hulchanski, J.D., & Shapcott, M. (Eds.). (2004). *Finding room: Policy options for a Canadian rental housing strategy*. Toronto: Centre of Urban and Community Studies Press, University of Toronto.

Human Resources and Skills Development Canada. (2011). *Federal disability report: Seniors with disabilities in Canada*. Gatineau, QC: Government of Canada.

Human Services Planning Coalition York Region. (2005). *The road to inclusivity: An action plan for York Region. Report of the Inclusivity Summit*. Newmarket, ON: York Region.

IBI Group. (2009). Ontario Ministry of Transportation 2008 travel time study. Toronto: IBI Group.

Ismail, M., & Smith, A. (2013). Evaluation report. Prepared for the Welcome Centres of York Region.

Jackson, K. (1985). *Crabgrass frontier: The suburbanization of the United States.* New York: Oxford University Press.

Jackson, K. (2006). Foreword. In B.M. Nicolaides & A. Wiese (Eds.), *The suburb reader* (pp. xxi–xxii). New York: Routledge.

Katz, B., & Lang, R.E. (2003). *Redefining urban and suburban America: Evidence from Census 2000.* Washington, DC: Brookings Institute Press.

Kazemipur, A., & Halli, S.S. (2000). *The new poverty in Canada: Ethnic groups and ghetto neighbourhoods.* Toronto: Thompson Educational Publishing.

Keil, R. (2002). "Common sense" neoliberalism: Progressive conservative urbanism in Toronto, Canada. *Antipode, 34*(3), 578–601. http://dx.doi.org/10.1111/1467-8330.00255

Keil, R., & Young, D. (2008). Transportation: The bottleneck of regional competitiveness in Toronto. *Environment and Planning. C, Government & Policy, 26*(4), 728–51. http://dx.doi.org/10.1068/c68m

Keil, R., & Young, D. (2009). Fringe explosions: Risk and vulnerability in Canada's new in-between urban landscape. *Canadian Geographer, 53*(4), 488–99.

Kenyon, S., Lyons, G., & Rafferty, J. (2002). Transport and social exclusion: Investigating the possibility of promoting inclusion through virtual mobility. *Journal of Transport Geography, 10*(3), 207–19. http://dx.doi.org/10.1016/S0966-6923(02)00012-1

Keung, N. (2011a, 23 February). Province, Ottawa battle over immigrant selection, settlement funds. *Toronto Star.* http://www.thestar.com/news/canada.html.

Keung, N. (2011b, 24 February).Dots on a map: Why newcomer funding is taking a hit. *Toronto Star.* http://www.thestar.com/news/canada.html.

Klausen, J.E., & Røe, P.G. (2012). Governance and change on the urban fringe. *Urban Research and Practice,* special issue, *5*(1), 1–5. http://dx.doi.org/10.1080/17535069.2012.656445

Kneebone, E., & Berube, A. (2013). *Confronting suburban poverty in America.* Washington, DC: Brookings Institution Press.

Kopun, F. (2007, 14 March). Boom beyond the 'burbs. *Toronto Star,* pp. A1, A14.

Kopun, F., & Keung, N. (2007, 5 December). A city of unmatched diversity: Many newcomers opt to bypass city, start new lives in suburbs surrounding Toronto. *Toronto Star,* p. A6.

Larner, W. (2000). Neo-liberalism: Policy, ideology, governmentality. *Studies in Political Economy, 63*, 5–25.

Lee, K. (2000). *Urban poverty in Canada: A statistical profile.* Ottawa: Canadian Council on Social Development.

Leitner, H., Peck, J., & Sheppard, E. (2007). *Contesting neoliberalism: Urban frontiers.* New York: Guidford.

Ley, D. (2010). *Millionaire migrants: Trans-Pacific life lines.* Malden, MA: Wiley-Blackwell. http://dx.doi.org/10.1002/9781444319262.

Ley, D., & Smith, H. (2000). Relations between deprivation and immigrant groups in large Canadian cities. *Urban Studies (Edinburgh, Scotland), 37*(1), 37–62. http://dx.doi.org/10.1080/0042098002285

Li, P.S. (2003). *Destination Canada: Immigration debates and issues.* Toronto: Oxford University Press.

Lim, A., Lo, L., Siemiatycki, M., & Doucet, M. (2005). *Newcomer services in the Greater Toronto Area: An exploration of the range and funding sources of settlement services.* Working Paper no. 35. Toronto: Centre of Excellence for Research on Immigration and Settlement.

Lo, L. (2011). Immigrants and social services in the suburbs. In D. Young, P.B. Wood, & R. Keil (Eds.), *In-between infrastructure: Urban connectivity in an age of vulnerability* (pp. 131–50). Praxis (e)Press.

Lo, L., Shalaby, A., & Alshalalfah, B. (2011). Case study: Relationship between immigrant settlement patterns and transit use in the Greater Toronto Area. *Journal of Urban Planning and Development, 137*(4), 470–6. http://dx.doi.org/10.1061/(ASCE)UP.1943-5444.0000080

Lo, L., Teixeira, C., & Truelove, M. (2002). *Cultural resources, ethnic strategies, and immigrant entrepreneurship: A comparative study of five immigrant groups in the Toronto CMA.* Working Paper Series no. 21. Toronto: Centre of Excellence for Research on Immigration and Settlement.

Lo, L., Wang, L., Wang, S., & Yuan, Y. (2007). *Immigrant settlement services in the Toronto CMA: A GIS-assisted analysis of demand and supply.* Working Paper Series no. 59. Toronto: Centre of Excellence for Research on Immigration and Settlement.

Lo, L., & Wang, S. (1997). Settlement patterns of Toronto's Chinese immigrants: Convergence or divergence? *Canadian Journal of Regional Science, 20*, 49–72.

Longley, P., & Clarke, G. (1995). *GIS for business and service planning.* Cambridge: Pearson Professional Ltd.

Lucas, K. (2004). Transport and social exclusion. In K. Lucas (Ed.), *Running on empty: Transport social exclusion and environmental justice* (pp. 39–53). Bristol, UK: Policy Press.

Lucy, W.H., & Phillips, D.L. (2000). *Confronting suburban decline: Strategic planning for metropolitan renewal*. Washington, DC: Island Press.

Lutz, M. (1994). Women immigrants and the New York human services system: Accommodation and acculturation. In V. Demos & E. Texler Segal (Eds.), *Ethnic women: A multiple status reality* (pp. 237–47). Dix Hills, NY: General Hall.

Marcelli, A. (2004). From the barrios to the 'burbs? Immigration and the dynamics of suburbanization. In J. Wolch, M. Pastor, & P. Dreier (Eds.), *Up against the sprawl: Public policy and the making of southern California* (pp. 123–50). Minneapolis, London: University of Minnesota Press.

McFarlane, C., & Rutherford, J. (2008). Political infrastructures: Governing and experiencing the fabric of the city. *International Journal of Urban and Regional Research, 32*(2), 363–74. http://dx.doi.org/10.1111/j.1468-2427.2008.00792.x

McLafferty, S. (1982). Urban structure and geographical access to public services. *Annals of the Association of American Geographers, 72*(3), 347–54. http://dx.doi.org/10.1111/j.1467-8306.1982.tb01830.x

McLafferty, S., & Preston, V. (1992). Spatial mismatch and labor market segmentation for African-American and Latina women. *Economic Geography, 68*(4), 406–31. http://dx.doi.org/10.2307/144026

Miller, E., & Shalaby, A. (2003). Evolution of person travel in the Toronto area & policy implications. *Journal of Urban Planning and Development, 129*(1), 1–26. http://dx.doi.org/10.1061/(ASCE)0733-9488(2003)129:1(1)

Millington, G. (2011). *"Race," culture, and the right to the city: Centres, peripheries, margins*. Basingstoke, UK: Palgrave Macmillan.

Millington, G. (2012). The outer-inner city: Urbanization, migration and "race" in London and New York. *Urban Research & Practice, 5*(1), 6–25. http://dx.doi.org/10.1080/17535069.2012.656447

Muller, P.O. (1981). *Contemporary suburban America*. Englewood Cliffs, NJ: Prentice-Hall.

Muller, P.O. (1997). The suburban transformation of the globalizing American city. *Annals of the American Academy of Political and Social Science, 551*(1), 44–58. http://dx.doi.org/10.1177/0002716297551001004

Murdie, R. (2008). *Diversity and concentration in Canadian immigration: Trends in Toronto, Montréal and Vancouver, 1971–2006*. Research Bulletin 42. Toronto: Centre for Urban and Community Studies / Cities Centre, University of Toronto.

Murdie, R., & Teixeira, C. (2003). Towards a comfortable neighbourhood and appropriate housing: immigrant experiences in Toronto. In P. Anisef & M. Lanphier (Eds.), *The world in a city* (pp. 132–91). Toronto: University of Toronto Press.

Murie, A., & Musterd, S. (2004). Social exclusion and opportunity structures in European cities and neighbourhoods. *Urban Studies (Edinburgh, Scotland)*, 41(8), 1441–59. http://dx.doi.org/10.1080/0042098042000226948

The National Seniors Council. (2009). *Report of the National Seniors Council on low income among seniors*. Ottawa: Government of Canada.

Nicolaides, B.M., & Wiese, A. (2006). *The suburb reader*. New York: Routledge.

OECD. (2010). *OECD territorial reviews: Toronto, Canada, 2009*. http://www.oecd-ilibrary.org/

Omidvar, R., & Richmond, T. (2003). *Immigrant settlement and social inclusion in Canada*. Toronto: Laidlaw Foundation.

Ornstein, M. (2006). *Ethno-racial groups in Toronto, 1971–2001: A demographical and socio-economic profile*. Toronto: Institute for Social Research, York University.

Peck, J. (2001). *Workfare states*. New York: Guilford Press.

Peck, J. (2010). *Constructions of neoliberal reason*. Oxford: Oxford University Press. http://dx.doi.org/10.1093/acprof:oso/9780199580576.001.0001.

Peck, J. (2011). Neoliberal suburbanism: Frontier space. *Urban Geography*, 32(6), 884–919. http://dx.doi.org/10.2747/0272-3638.32.6.884

Peck, J., & Tickell, A. (2002). Neoliberalizing space. *Antipode*, 34(3), 380–404. http://dx.doi.org/10.1111/1467-8330.00247

Pembina Institute. (2007). *Ontario community sustainability report, 2007*.

Percy-Smith, J. (2000). Introduction: The contours of social exclusion. In J. Percy-Smith (Ed.), *Policy responses to social exclusion: Towards inclusion?* (pp. 1–21. Buckingham, UK: Open University Press.

Phelps, N.A., & Wu, F. (Eds.). (2011). *International perspectives on suburbanization: A post-suburban world?* New York: Palgrave Macmillan. http://dx.doi.org/10.1057/9780230308626

Picot, G. (2008). *Immigrant economic and social outcomes in Canada: Research and data development at Statistics Canada*. Research Paper Series, catalogue no. 11F0019M — No. 319. Ottawa: Statistics Canada, Analytical Studies Branch.

Picot, G., & Hou, F. (2003). *The rise in low-income rates among immigrants in Canada*. Ottawa: Statistics Canada, Analytical Studies Branch.

Picot, G., Hou, F., & Coulombe, S. (2008). Poverty dynamics among recent immigrants to Canada. *International Migration Review*, 42(2), 393–424. http://dx.doi.org/10.1111/j.1747-7379.2008.00129.x

Polonsky, L. (2011). *Development of the York Regional Transportation Master Plan: Final report*. Newmarket, ON: York Region.

Prentice, J. (2009). *2006 Census housing series: Issue 2, The geography of core housing need, 2001–2006. Research Highlights, Socio-economic Series 09–005*. Ottawa: Canada Mortgage and Housing Corporation.

Preston, V., Lo, L., & Wang, S. (2003). Immigrants' economic status in Toronto: Stories of triumph and disappointment. In P. Anisef & M. Lanphier (Eds.), *The world in a city* (pp. 192–262). Toronto: University of Toronto Press.

Preston, V., & McLafferty, S. (1999). Spatial mismatch research in the 1990s: Progress and potential. *Papers in Regional Science, 78*(4), 387–402. http:// dx.doi.org/10.1007/s101100050033

Preston, V., Murdie, R., Wedlock, J., Agrawal, S., Anucha, U., D'Addario, S., …, & Murnaghan, A.M. (2009). Immigrants and homelessness – At risk in Canada's outer suburbs. *Canadian Geographer, 53*(3), 288–304. http://dx.doi .org/10.1111/j.1541-0064.2009.00264.x

PricewaterhouseCoopers LLP. (2006). *Assessing the gap in health and social service funding between the GTA/905 and the rest of Ontario: A report prepared for Strong Communities Coalition, a coalition of human services in Durham.* Halton, Peel, and York Regions.

Regional Municipality of York. (2006). *Employment and industry 2006, York Region.* Newmarket, ON: York Region.

Reitz, J. (1995). *A review of the literature on aspects of ethno-racial access, utilization and delivery of social services.* Report prepared as a joint project of the Multicultural Coalition for Access to Family Services, Toronto, and the Ontario Ministry of Community and Social Services. Toronto: Multicultural Coalition for Access to Family Services and Government of Ontario.

Richmond, T., & Saloojee, A. (2005). *Social inclusion: Canadian perspectives.* Toronto: Fernwood.

Roeher Institute. (2003). *Policy approaches to framing social inclusion and social exclusion: An overview.* Toronto: Roeher Institute.

Rose, D., Germain, A., Bacqué, M.-H., Bridge, G., Fijalkow, Y., & Slater, T. (2013). "Social mix" and neighbourhood revitalization in a transatlantic perspective: Comparing local policy discourses and expectations in Paris (France), Bristol (UK), and Montréal (Canada). *International Journal of Urban and Regional Research, 37*(2), 430–50. http://dx.doi. org/10.1111/j.1468-2427.2012.01127.x

Sadiq, K. (2004). *The two-tier settlement system: A review of current newcomer settlement services in Canada.* Working Paper no. 34.Toronto: Centre of Excellence for Research on Immigration and Settlement.

Sandercock, L. (2003). *Cosmopolis II: Mongrel cities of the 21st century.* London: Continuum.

Schellenberg, G., & Maheux, H. (2007). Immigrants' perspectives on their first four years in Canada: Highlights from three waves of the Longitudinal Survey of Immigrants to Canada. *Canadian Social Trends,* (Special edition): 2–34.

Sen, A. (2001). *Development as freedom*. London: Oxford University Press.

Sewell, J. (2009). *Shape of the suburbs: Understanding Toronto's sprawl*. Toronto: University of Toronto Press.

Sharma, R.D. (2012). *Poverty in Canada*. Toronto: Oxford University Press.

Silverstone, R. (1997). *Visions of suburbia*. New York: Routledge.

Smoyer-Tomic, K.E., Hewko, J.N., & Hodgson, M.J. (2004). Spatial accessibility and equity of playgrounds in Edmonton, Canada. *Canadian Geographer, 48*(3), 287–302. http://dx.doi.org/10.1111/j.0008-3658.2004.00061.x

Snowden, L.R., Hu, T.-W., & Jerrell, J.M. (1995). Emergency care avoidance: Ethnic matching and participation in minority-serving programs. *Community Mental Health Journal, 31*(5), 463–73. http://dx.doi.org/10.1007/BF02188616

Special Priority Policy Research Task Force. (2011). *SPP impact study, phase 1, step 1: Impact review of the Special Priority Policy for Victims of Domestic Abuse, Applying for Assisted Housing – Outcomes*. June. Available at http://www.hscorp.ca/resources/spp-impact-study/.

Stanilov, K., & Scheer, B.C. (2004). *Suburban Form: An International Perspective*. New York: Routledge.

Statistics Canada. (1983).

Statistics Canada. (1993).

Statistics Canada. (2003). *Custom tabulations from the 2001 Census*. Toronto: Statistics Canada Office.

Statistics Canada. (2005a). Low income cut-offs for 2006 and low income measures for 2005. Income Research Paper Series, catalogue no. 75F0002MIE, no. 004. Ottawa: Statistics Canada.

Statistics Canada. (2005b). Profile of census divisions and subdivisions, 1996 Census. Catalogue no. 95F0181XDB96001. Released 26 April. Ottawa: Statistics Canada. http://www12.statcan.gc.ca/english/census96/data/profiles/Index-eng.cfm

Statistics Canada. (2006). Cumulative profile, 2006 – Ont., 2006 Census of population (provinces, census divisions, municipalities). http://ezproxy.library.yorku.ca/cgi-win/cnsmcgi.exe?Lang=E&EST-Fi=EStat

Statistics Canada. (2007a). *2006 Community profile. 2006 Census*. Statistics Canada catalogue no. 92–591-XWE. Released 13 March. Ottawa. http://www12.statcan.ca/census-recensement/2006/dp-pd/prof/92-591/index.cfm?Lang=E

Statistics Canada. (2007b). *Custom tabulations from the 2001 Census – EO1048–3A*. Toronto: Statistics Canada Office.

Statistics Canada. (2007c). *Portrait of the Canadian population in 2006*. Catalogue no. 97–550-XIE. Ottawa: Ministry of Industry.

Statistics Canada. (2008). *Custom tabulations from the 2006 Census – EO1204R–2*. Toronto: Statistics Canada Office.

Statistics Canada. (2012a). *The Canadian population in 2011: Population counts and growth*. Ottawa: Ministry of Industry.

Statistics Canada. (2012b). *Census profile: 2011 Census*. Statistics Canada, catalogue no. 98–316-XWE. Ottawa. Released 24 October. Accessed 13 March 2013, http://www12.statcan.gc.ca/census-recensement/2011/dp-pd/prof/index.cfm?Lang=E.

Sue, S., Fujino, D.C., Hu, L.T., Takeuchi, D.T., & Zane, N.W.S. (1991). Community mental health services for ethnic minority groups: A test of the cultural responsiveness hypothesis. *Journal of Consulting and Clinical Psychology, 59*(4), 533–40. http://dx.doi.org/10.1037/0022-006X.59.4.533

Suttor, G.L. (2007). *Growth management and affordable housing in Greater Toronto: A macro view of Toronto social mix and polarization*. Research report. Ottawa: Canada Mortgage and Housing Corporation.

Taylor, L. (2011). No boundaries: Exurbia and the study of contemporary urban dispersion. *GeoJournal 76*(4), 323–39.

Teaford, J.C. (2008). *The American suburbs: The basics*. New York: Routledge.

Teaford, J.C. (2011). Suburbia and post-suburbia: A brief history. In N.A. Phelps & F. Wu (Eds.), *International perspectives on suburbanization: A post-suburban world?* (pp. 15–34). New York: Palgrave Macmillan. http://dx.doi.org/10.1057/9780230308626.0009.

Teixeira, C., Li, W., & Kobayashi, A. (2011). *Immigrant geographies in North American cities*. Toronto: Oxford University Press.

Torrance, M.I. (2008). Forging glocal governance? Urban infrastructures as networked financial products. *International Journal of Urban and Regional Research, 32*(1), 1–21. http://dx.doi.org/10.1111/j.1468-2427.2007.00756.x

Townson, M. (2006). *Growing older, working longer: The new face of retirement*. Ottawa: Canadian Centre for Policy Alternatives.

Truelove, M. (2000). Services for immigrant women: An evaluation of locations. *Canadian Geographer, 44*(2), 135–51. http://dx.doi.org/10.1111/j.1541-0064.2000.tb00698.x

Turcotte, M., & Ruel, J. (2008). *Commuting patterns and places of work of Canadians, 2006 Census*. Statistics Canada Research Report. Ottawa: Ministry of Industry.

Turner, S. (2008). *Mediating the privatization of social housing in York Region, Ontario: The role of civil society*. (MA thesis). Graduate Programme in Geography, York University, Toronto.

United Way of Greater Toronto and The Canadian Council on Social Development. (2004). *Poverty by postal code: The geography of neighbourhood poverty, City of Toronto, 1981–2001*. Toronto: United Way of Greater Toronto.

Vertovec, S. (2007). Super-diversity and its implications. *Ethnic and Racial Studies, 30*(6), 1024–54. http://dx.doi.org/10.1080/01419870701599465

Walks, R.A. (2011). Economic restructuring and trajectories of socio-spatial polarization in the twenty-first-century Canadian city. In L.S. Bourne, T. Hutton, R. Shearmur, & J. Simmons (Eds.), *Canadian urban regions: Trajectories of growth and change* (pp. 125–59). Toronto: Oxford University Press.

Wang, L., Rosenberg, M., & Lo, L. (2008). Ethnicity and utilization of family physicians: A case study of mainland Chinese immigrants in Toronto, Canada. *Social Science & Medicine, 67*(9), 1410–22. http://dx.doi.org/10.1016/j.socscimed.2008.06.012

Wang, S., & Truelove, M. (2003). Evaluation of settlement service programs for newcomers in Ontario: A geographical perspective. *Journal of International Migration and Integration, 4*(4), 577–606. http://dx.doi.org/10.1007/s12134-003-1015-1

Wayland, S. (2011). *A case study of the Local Immigration Partnership model.* Unpublished paper.

Weiss, D. (2003). *Social exclusion: An approach to the Australian case.* New York: P. Lang.

Whitzman, C. (2006). At the intersection of invisibilities: Canadian women, homelessness, and health outside the "big city." *Gender, Place and Culture, 13*(4), 383–99. http://dx.doi.org/10.1080/09663690600808502

Willett, G. (2003). Social exclusion and gay and lesbian people. In D. Weiss (Ed.), *Social exclusion: An approach to the Australian case.* New York: P. Lang.

Wolch, J., Pastor, M., Jr., & Dreier, P. (2004). *Up against the sprawl: Public policy and the making of southern California.* Minneapolis: University of Minnesota Press.

Wu, I.-H., & Windle, C. (1980). Ethnic specificity in the relative minority use and staffing of community mental health centers. *Community Mental Health Journal, 16*(2), 156–68. http://dx.doi.org/10.1007/BF00778587

York Region. (2001). *Human services strategy: Final report.* Newmarket, ON: York Region.

York Region. (2004). *Employer opinion survey.* Newmarket, ON: York Region.

York Region. (2006). Department of Geomatics. Spatial data files of York Region provided to the research team.

York Region. (2007). *Housing by the numbers.* Newmarket, ON: Community Services and Housing Department.

York Region. (2009). *Employment and industry 2009.* Newmarket, ON: York Region.

York Region. (2010). *Employment and industry 2010.* Newmarket, ON: York Region.

York Region Planning and Development Services Department. (2007). *Economic and development review 2007.* Newmarket, ON: York Region.

York Region Planning and Development Services Department. (2008). *Economic and development review.* Newmarket, ON: York Region.

York Regional Council Meeting. (2008). *Report no. 6 of the Transit Committee.* 16 September.

York Region Human Services Planning Coalition. (2003). *Towards a new model for social services funding of York Region.* Newmarket, ON: York Region.

York Region Human Services Planning Coalition. (2007). *English language programs study: Addressing the language needs of new immigrants to York Region.* Newmarket, ON: York Region.

Young, D., & Keil, R. (2010). Reconnecting the disconnected: The politics of infrastructure in the in-between city. *Cities, 27*(2), 87–95.

Young, D., Wood, P.B., & Keil, R. (2011). *In-between infrastructure: Urban connectivity in an age of vulnerability.* Praxis (e)Press.

Index

The letter *f* following a page number denotes a figure; the letter *t* a table; and the letter *n* a note on that page.